DO-IT-YOURSELF BOOK SIGNING

The Chaser writers couldn't be arsed attending poncey book signings. But if these things are important to you, we give you full permission to forge our signatures in the space provided below.

To: _____

[insert your name here]

_____

[insert optional patronising homily here]

_____

[insert illegible signature scrawl here]

And there you have it – your very own personally signed copy of *The Chaser Annual*! With none of the fuss of having to queue up at an arty inner-city bookshop.

* If any readers would still prefer a genuine author's signature, then please mail your book to Jeffrey Archer, c/o Her Majesty's Pleasure, England. He's agreed to sign all books on our behalf, given he's got so much time on his hands.

[*Note: genuine Archer signature may diminish value of book.*]

What the critics said about
THE CHASER ANNUAL

'I loved it'
David Stratton

'I hated it'
Margaret Pomeranz

'Well, what would you know anyway?'
David Stratton

'A fat lot more than you, arsewipe'
Margaret Pomeranz

'Bitch'
David Stratton

'Cunt'
Margaret Pomeranz

The Chaser
Annual
2002

TEXT PUBLISHING
MELBOURNE AUSTRALIA

The Text Publishing Company
171 La Trobe Street
Melbourne Victoria 3000
Australia

Most of the articles in *The Chaser Annual* were first published in *The Chaser* newspaper.

This edition published 2002, reprinted 2002

Printed and bound by Adams Printers
Designed and typeset by Natalie Matheson

ISBN 1 877008 33 8
ISSN 1445-9094

DISCLAIMER

The Chaser is committed to avoiding litigation in all areas other than defamation. With the recent explosion of negligence claims in the courts, we have received legal advice to include a more specific warning with *The Chaser Annual* for protection against liability for risks that plaintiff lawyers might say we should have foreseen.

Before proceeding further all readers are asked to carefully read the following warning, which lists some of the risks that may be associated with reading *The Chaser*. While every effort has been made to be comprehensive, there may be some eventualities which are not specifically referred to below. Readers are invited to submit any risks which are not listed below to editor@chaser.com.au.

Pre-warning warning: The following warning may take some time to review. *The Chaser* recommends that before starting you sit down, very carefully, in a comfortable and safe environment. Maintain good posture at all times while reading, and take regular breaks for food and exercise as required or as directed by your doctor.

Warning:

The Chaser newspaper may cause paper cuts. Readers are advised to take care when turning each page and in particular to avoid aggressive rubbing of the edges of sheets of *The Chaser* against the skin of yourself, any other person or living thing. In order to reduce the risk of paper cuts, you might consider not turning to pages 5, 11, 17 and 20 which – be warned – are generally of lower standard and have been known to induce pain in some cases.

Please avoid mixing *The Chaser* with water and glue, which could result in the inadvertent creation of a papier maché formula that could set, especially if exposed to the sun, which is not recommended, and may cause some readers to be caught in a papier maché death trap.

To avoid any damage to the eyes when reading *The Chaser*, make sure that the place you are reading in is well lit. If the light is inadequate, do not use matches or any other form of naked flame to increase visibility. It is also not impossible that some form of aggressive insect or other dangerous projectile could come into contact with your eyes while reading *The Chaser*. Goggles or other forms of protective eyewear are therefore recommended, provided they are made from shatter-proof glass and comply with Australian Standard AS566244763LFD4, all international treaties that are or may become binding on Australia and the Universal Declaration of Human Rights.

The humorous material contained within *The Chaser* is prepared by experts and placed in a particular context to render it safe for domestic use. Removing particular jokes and attempting to use them in any other format, whether by repeating them to another person or using them in another publication may cause embarrassment, social awkwardness, long, difficult-to-manage pauses and the perception amongst others that (i) you are a bit of an over-educated leftie tosser or (ii) you are getting all your good gags from people who, let's face it, pay the bills by taking money from Triple M.

Readers should consider the political environment before obtaining or reading *The Chaser*. Use of *The Chaser* is not recommended in places ruled by foreign regimes that restrict freedom of speech, or Queensland.

If reading *The Chaser* at the beach, avoid consuming excessive amounts of alcohol and swimming, whether between the flags or otherwise, in areas which may result in spinal injury.

Do not read *The Chaser* while driving.

Do not read *The Chaser* in a car which has all doors and windows closed and is exposed to direct sunlight or other heat. If leaving an infant unattended in a locked car, do not leave *The Chaser* with the child or anywhere in the car.

Do not commit suicide while reading *The Chaser*.

Do not read *The Chaser* in the presence of Doug Moran or any member of his family.

If any part of *The Chaser* causes disagreement between you and any other person, the editors recommend that disputes be resolved without recourse to violence. If a dispute concerning a *Chaser* article cannot be resolved without physical aggression, combatants are advised to fight only at locations that have valid and paid-up public liability insurance and/or in playgrounds administered by the Department of Education or another public body. Fights should be conducted in the presence of a qualified referee and with medical help readily available. No biting, scratching, blows below the belt or nipple cripples.

In the unlikely event that you are caused to laugh while reading *The Chaser*, even if it is because of something unconnected with the content of the newspaper, readers are advised to laugh in moderation. Laughing persons should take special care to ensure that their sides remain intact and should seek urgent medical attention if any signs of splitting develop. Do not read *The Chaser* if either you or a relative has previously died from laughing.

The Chaser is not suitable for human consumption. It should not be eaten or used to wrap foodstuffs. The publishers of *The Chaser* strongly recommend against using *The Chaser* to wrap any food, including fish and chips. If swallowed, sit the victim in a cool place out of the direct sun, and monitor. Induce vomiting if and only if under proper medical supervision and you feel it would be mildly amusing to you to watch the victim vomit.

The Chaser is flammable. Do not set fire to your copy of *The Chaser*, whether with a match, cigarette lighter, soaking it in petrol, rubbing two or more sticks together, shining a magnifying glass on a particular little spot or by storing your copy of *The Chaser* in the nuclear furnace that is the heart of the Sun. If you choose to smoke while reading your copy of *The Chaser*, the publishers accept no responsibility for any loss or damage arising to you in exercising that choice. Never attempt to use *The Chaser* to extinguish a fire. If your copy of *The Chaser* catches fire, please return it by placing the flaming copy in an envelope, together with a stamped self-addressed envelope for return, and sending it to the address shown in the publisher's notice above.

The Chaser is not a flotation device. Should your copy of *The Chaser* become wet, it may become soggy and unsuitable for using when all the Tally-Hos have run out.

Using *The Chaser* in place of your regular toilet tissue is not sanctioned by the publishers of *The Chaser*. Such use can result in nicks and cuts in awkward, hard-to-reach places and cause irritation, grumpiness and, in the event of becoming distracted by a news-story during such use, unexpected or unwanted faecal smearing.

Special care should be taken when reading *The Chaser* in circumstances where young children could be exposed to humorous or satirical content. *The Chaser* is not responsible for any damage that may occur to children or children's behaviour patterns as a result of poorly supervised access to *The Chaser* up to and including: believing that it is funny to send rude letters to prominent people you don't know; taking money from John Singleton; thinking that it is 'clever' or 'cool' to shill your own brand on the ABC; using the word 'fuck' in any print medium where the term 'f---' would be a perfectly accepted and *Sydney Morning Herald* Style Guide approved substitute; using unacceptable or un-Parliamentary language such as 'piss-flaps', 'poo-hole', 'spadger' or 'Satan's little battery'.

Do not apply *The Chaser* internally. Specifically, readers are warned that they should not roll up *The Chaser*, lube it, and perform the ritual known colloquially as 'the Paddy McGuinness' on themselves or any other person (Oh, all right then, but for goodness sake don't tell anyone).

Do not use *The Chaser* for birth control. We will not take responsibility for anything which may occur as a result of attempting to use *The Chaser* for birth control including; children, awkward moments during sexual contact or inability to read *Chaser* articles due to jism stains.

The Chaser is not designed to be used as a parachute. Any similarity between the design of *The Chaser* and a parachute is merely coincidental. We will not be held responsible for any plummeting into the earth which occurs whilst holding *The Chaser* above your head and jumping from a plane.

We will not be held responsible for the death or sickness of any vagrants, bums, derelicts, tramps, beggars, drifters, beatniks, hobos or unemployed Japanese career men who use *The Chaser* as a blanket, home, shelter, refuge, haven or source of satire.

The Chaser should not be used as a substitute for education, even for those attending public, second rate Catholic or Seventh Day Adventist schools. Reading *The Chaser* does not eliminate the need for proper education and may actually increase this need. Failure to complete homework due to the reading of *The Chaser* is not our fault. Any lack of reading or writing ability which occurs later in life is the fault of the reader. The Department of Education in your state should be sued for this fault and not the proprietors of *The Chaser* nor those who shield *The Chaser* proprietors' assets.

The Chaser should not be used for deep sea rescue. Nor should it be read to airline passengers in place of warnings regarding the fastening and releasing of seatbelts.

Avoid any persons who claim that *The Chaser* can be made into a trampoline. If made into a trampoline we will not take any responsibility.

The Chaser should not be read while tipping a fridge on yourself. (See fridge for more specific warning pertaining to this cause of litigation.)

If reading *The Chaser* in the United States of America you must wear a helmet which meets the latest standards set by the National Operating Committee on Standards for Athletic Equipment. We will not be held responsible for any injury sustained as a result of faults in the helmet or which may occur due to being tackled because of your wearing of the helmet.

Avant-garde fashion designers should not use *The Chaser* in the design of their clothes. We will not be held responsible for any loss of earnings or reputation which result from the inability of your audience to understand that your use of our daggy newspaper was meant to be a post-modern ironic statement.

Do not shred *The Chaser* and use it as confetti. *The Chaser* will not be held responsible for any kitchness which may occur at weddings or other ceremonies which utilise *The Chaser* as confetti. We make no guarantees as to the longevity of any marital unions formed whilst using *The Chaser* in any part of the ceremony whether as decorations or in place of a purpose built drop-sheet or bin-liner.

The Chaser warns against the reading of large tracts of small text. We will not be held responsible for poor eyesight or disappointment in the search for humour that you may sustain from reading such large tracts of text.

ABOUT THE AUTHOR

SEDGEWICK J. CLYTE

Sedgewick J. Clyte was born in 1954, and later again in 1963. He grew up in Sri Lanka, where his childhood experiences formed the basis of his first book *Paris: A City Guide.* After moving to England, Clyte worked as a political journalist for *The Times, The New Statesman* and the Damart winter catalogue. His first book of essays, misleadingly titled *Second Book Of Essays*, was described by one influential critic as 'a book'. For his follow-up, Clyte hired an old castle in France and teamed up with legendary producers Phil Spector and Nigel Godrich, who later advised him they knew nothing about books. In 1988 he was appointed Writer in Residence at his own bedsit apartment. During this period he was instrumental in founding Most-Podernism, a new movement for pretentious dyslexics. Despite its acclaim, Clyte soon fell out of favour with the literary establishment after holding a literary luncheon during dinner hours. Last year he published a controversial book of letters, which included 'b', 'l' and 'w'. His books have been translated into fourteen different languages, except for his seminal English Dictionary, which is still only available in Italian.

The author gratefully acknowledges the assistance of Andrew Bliss, Scott Dooley, James Edwards, Johanna Featherstone, Charles Firth, Joel Gibson, Kara Greiner, Andrew Hansen, Fiona Katauskas, Dominic Knight, Chas Licciardello, Arion McNicoll, Julian Morrow, Lisa Pryor, Craig Reucassel, Dave Stewart, Chris Taylor, Matt Taylor, Mark Thomson, Oliver Watts and Andrew Weldon in producing this book.

Additional plagiarism by former Monash University's former Vice-Chancellor David Robinson.

CONTENTS

FOREWORD
Laurie Oakes

This book is a sham. A lie. A total distortion of history. The authors purport to present the full story. But how can it be a credible account, when the writers fail to mention their big secret? I won't say what the 'big secret' is – I've got far too much journalistic integrity for that. Oh, all right then – I'll tell you. Or should I drop innuendos a little bit longer, then come out right with it when I have a bigger audience on Channel Nine? To hell with it – these authors have had sex. Filthy philanderers, the lot of them! Root merchants. Trouser lads. How can they live with themselves being so unethical? I know I couldn't.

Here then, purely in the interests of political discourse, let me tell you all about their sex lives. Let me give you every steamy detail of

(Saliva stains render rest of foreword illegible – Ed.)

Laurie Oakes
Canberra
October 2002

INTRODUCTION

The directors of *The Chaser* would like to make it clear they were completely unaware of the financial mismanagement that has seen *The Chaser* placed into voluntary administration.

When we floated *The Chaser* in June 2000, it was valued at $12 million. Our prospectus promised blue sky growth, tapping into the New Economy's latest craze for satirical print newspapers. If nothing else, the spin-off merchandising possibilities seemed endless: witty T-shirts and coffee mugs, and those hilarious signs which say 'You don't have to be crazy to work here, but it helps.'

Unfortunately, it didn't play out quite as planned. The revenue from satirical newspaper merchandising did not outstrip the total combined sales of the world's manufacturing industry in the first year, as projected. Still, we stand by our initial projections – at the time they seemed prudent, and even conservative. How were we to know that cars and fridges weren't just a passing fad?

By October this year, we had lost $3 billion of investors' money. Luckily, most of that money came directly from the superannuation funds of baby boomers – so it doesn't really affect us.

You may wonder how a small satirical newspaper that only sells a few thousand copies each fortnight could possibly lose $3 billion in just over two years. But you must realise there were significant unavoidable costs. Generous executive remuneration packages were necessary to keep key directors in an increasingly competitive satirical sector. These were kept as low as absolutely possible and only account for a couple of billion dollars worth of losses.

And again, we would like to repeat that the stock options packages – which made all the directors paper billionaires despite a falling share price – were done at no cost to *The Chaser*, which stuck strictly to the letter of all accounting standards as laid down by our accountants (Andersen), and endorsed by our auditors (Andersen).

As for the loans to directors, they are easily explained. It is not unusual for cash-strapped companies to loan their directors money to buy shares to prop up the company. It may be illegal, but it's certainly not unusual. Besides, our financial consultants (Andersen) didn't see anything wrong with it, and they were the ones – not us – to suggest we use the company's stock as collateral for the loans.

But perhaps the biggest shock this year came in September when it was revealed that *The Chaser* had bought all of its own existing shares in an attempt to keep the share price up. This meant that *The Chaser* had no owner and was on the brink of self-imploding in a financial feedback loop. Luckily an owner emerged, and we're proud that a man of Brad Cooper's stature is now associated so closely with *The Chaser*.

There is some positive news. Our cash burn rate – currently $107 million per month – is projected to level out by the end of next year, mainly because we don't expect to be in business by the end of next year.

Finally, let me make this absolutely clear: neither the directors, nor anyone else running the company has ever known what was going on with the company's finances. We were provided with statements by our Chief Financial Officer (Jules) and when we asked him whether they were true and correct, he told us 'Yes, and there is no need for you to investigate further.' Simply put, if anything seems our fault, it is only because we were profoundly misled. Julian is a great friend and colleague of all of us, and I wish him well in his impending criminal proceedings. I hope our testimony against him does not sour our working relationship.

Needless to say, we're not proud of being so oblivious to the strange financial wizardry that went on in our company, but we honestly did not know about it. The reason we all sold our stock in the weeks leading up to *The Chaser*'s bankruptcy was for individual, personal reasons, and not because we knew what was going on inside the company. The emails that purport to show otherwise have been taken completely out of context.

We look forward to defending our version of events in the upcoming Royal Commission into our collapse, and we hope that all the facts come out.

The Directors, November 2002

Witnessed by: _____

9th October 2001

Greens quietly unconfident about forming government

HOBART, Monday: A leaked memo from a senior member of the Greens reveals the party is unconfident of winning government on November 10. The memo exposes massive self-doubt in the Greens ranks about the viability of seizing power.

A spokesman for the Greens wouldn't reveal the source of the memo, but did confirm that the mood of the party was currently pessimistic. He said a recent poll which measured support for the Greens at just 1.8% had severely dented the party's hopes of forming government.

'Many of our candidates have virtually resigned themselves to the idea they can't win,' the spokesman said. 'Bob Brown himself has stopped talking about himself as a future Prime Minister. In fact, morale is so low at the moment we're not even confident of forming an Opposition.'

Bathurst V8 Supercar 1000 marred by double demerit points

HOW TO SURVIVE THE WAR™ GUIDE ®

Welcome to the

STRESSED?   TIRED?   ANXIOUS?

All you need is *The Chaser*'s How to Survive the War™ Guide®

★ ★ ★ ★ ★

With a minimum of fuss, we show you all the HOTTEST TIPS for surviving the war between evil Afghanistan and the rest of the world.

1 Our patented War Eliminator™ spray

WAR PROBLEMS?

Let War Eliminator's™ all-natural ingredients keep you safe.

Is war keeping you up all night? No more sleepless nights with War Eliminator™!

Let your family rest easy again by using War Eliminator™

Do you know someone with a world war problem? War Eliminator™ will help them, and they will love you for it.

Improve your sexual performance by reducing warfare and thus increasing the tiny endorphins of happiness in your brain!

People who engage in wars have a HIGHER RISK of developing heart attacks, high blood pressure, strokes, and disembowelment. Warfare also causes sleep disturbances that lead to increased anxiety, irritability, and decreased memory.

Individuals who wage wars have a 90% chance of daytime fatigue. And 99 out of every 100 victims are male!

The hidden dangers of warfare

[This section to be read aloud in the voice of John Laws]

Warfare can cause problems with your house, car and lifestyle, as bombs and missiles are over 98% likely to destroy your entire street upon impact.

That's why we developed the War Eliminator™ spray. We recommend you commence your preparations for war by using our handy War Eliminator™ spray on all your furnishings as well as your ceiling, walls, garden, and driveway.

Secret fibres in the War Eliminator™ spray help to strengthen the bonds between the molecules of your home environment so they will be resistant to extermination by bombs and missiles.

Not only this, but blended into the spray, a soothing mix of aloe vera, sea kelp and banana helps to cool down the fiery emotions of Afghans who may be snooping around your home. In a matter of moments, they will stop thinking fanatically about Allah and murder, and begin to feel gentle and comfortable, just like a normal person.

What's more, War Eliminator™ comes in four attractive fragrances! Select your favourite from Truth™, Justice™, Bravery™, and Lemon.

End of the World™!

WORLD WAR III OCCURRING? NO PROBLEM!™

★ ★ ★ ★ ★

Only our authentic Guide® gives you ALL the information you need to play your part in DESTROYING the Afghans while at the same time PROTECTING yourself, your family, and your wallet!

2 Prepare your home

BOMB SHELTERS are large, complicated, and expensive.

The good news is: You don't need to build a bomb shelter! Why not? Because one of your neighbours will have built one already, like the cowardly, quivering puppy they are.

In case of a bomb, missile, or air raid attack, simply utilise your neighbour's bomb shelter ... It is important to arrive at their shelter before they do, so make haste! Once you and your family are safely inside, lock and seal its big, bulky door.

You may hear blood-curdling shrieks from your neighbour and his or her family as they scratch desperately at the massive door in an absurd attempt to enter the usurped bunker. Nothing a little planning can't fix – make sure you've brought your portable stereo into the shelter! You can then use merry songs to drown out their squeals.

★ ★ ★ ★ ★

NOTE: If your neighbours reach the shelter before you do, simply stand outside it and shout, 'It's okay! It was a false alarm! You can come out! Thank God for that! I can't believe it!'

You may also need to laugh convincingly as if having obtained a new lease of life. Then when your neighbours emerge, rush inside the shelter and seal it behind you, leaving them to be vaporised.

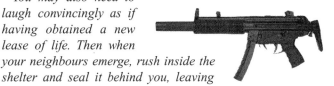

What causes war?

★ **Laziness**

★ **Excessive fat**

★ **Grumpiness**

★ **Afghans**

Heavy warfare is often associated with anger, or the stopping of niceness. As an individual goes through the day, his or her niceness gets disrupted and fragmented due to inconvenient things happening, such as having his or her entire culture and history rendered extinct by American market forces.

★ ★ ★ ★ ★

This can be a very hazardous problem if someone is not getting enough money. Warfare is the visible symptom of a small wallet.

★ ★ ★ ★ ★

Warfare is also more likely to occur between people who hate each other.

Welcome to the

Testimonials from our valued customers

'I am having a good night's sleep, finally! I used to wake myself up during the night worrying about the end of the world, but now that I know War Eliminator™ is keeping my house and family safe, I am completely fulfilled and content and want nothing more out of life ever again! P.S. My husband loves it as much as I do!'
— **Meg, Texas.***

'In April 1997, I was diagnosed with severe warfare. Doctors recommended I quit the army. I did so, but I still took myself about butchering people with a machete. Then I discovered War Eliminator™. I sprayed it all around my house and under my arms, and now I'm a sweet, generous, loving person with a wife, two children and a beagle.'
— **Alexyov, Bosnia.***

FOOD

YOU MUST HOARD appropriate food for the war, in case you need to live in the bomb shelter. This is important, as having no food during your two-year stay in the shelter will cause your energy levels to lag.

★ ★ ★ ★ ★

For every year you plan to spend in the shelter, each member of your family should take in 185 kg of fruit and vegetables, 70 kg of cereals, 120 kg of meat and fish, 175 kg of dairy products, and 175 kg of miscellaneous foodstuffs.

★ ★ ★ ★ ★

A nice trick you can play on the Middle Eastern enemy is to spitefully hoard hundreds of doner kebabs — not only will you create a food shortage in their community, but you can eat the kebabs defiantly while in your shelter for the next two years!

***** Customers guaranteed to not exist.**

End of the World™!
★ AMERICAN FRIENDS ★

ONCE THE WAR is nicely under way, you may need to cope with some awkwardness or embarrassment when broaching the subject with any American friends you may accidentally have who live in Australia.

Here are some fun suggestions for bonding with such American friends while the war is taking place!

Invite the Americans around for an afternoon of effigy making. This is a fun and easy way to spend quality time together. Simply wind some rags around a couple of broomsticks to make a sort of person, then cloak it in a dressing gown and wrap a towel around its head. Stick a false wicked-looking beard on its raggy face, and voilà! A pretend Afghan. Now, insisting that your American friends accompany you, proceed with some cans of petrol, a match, and your effigy to the nearest kebab shop. Here, douse both the effigy and the shop staff in petrol, and set fire to both. It's so easy! You may wish to chip in with a cutting remark or two at the bellowing shopkeepers, such as 'Look! A human kebab,' or 'Not winning the war now, are we, kebab-chefs?'

Cheer up your American friends by performing a huge benefit concert to raise money for American victims of this sneaky, terrorist war. If you are not a famous musician, do not worry. Simply contact your local television stations and insist that they place you in a stadium and broadcast you singing shakily along to your favourite songs with a backing track, while holding phone lines open for people willing to donate. If the television stations do not comply with your wishes, you should affect an American accent and say to them, 'But I'm an American. Are you Australians not helping me?' Their shameful lack of patriotism to America now threatened with exposure, the stations' public relations staff will immediately provide you with an unlimited budget to do whatever you please!

In the next issue...

We show you:

How to convince Afghanistan to hand over Osama bin-Laden to the USA using ordinary household items

★ ★ ★ ★ ★

How to restrain yourself from mentioning in conversations that you yourself once visited the World Trade Center

★ ★ ★ ★ ★

How to shop at late-night convenience stores and kebab joints without awkwardness, and

★ ★ ★ ★ ★

How to distinguish a mosque from a decent, Christian church.

Special Arms-Length Retaliation Feature

The Armchair-General's

As the world stood shocked on September 11, a new war was launched. A war without borders, or armies. A war that our armed forces must fight without the comfort of a defined battlefield, or clear lines of accountability, or the 1976 Presidential Order banning state-sponsored assassinations by the US.

Prosecuting to completion a war on terror that eliminates the ability of all terrorist organisations 'of global reach' to operate effectively could take some time, extending across all continents, throughout the world and into both ratings and non-ratings periods. It is, however, confusing to the lay-viewer. Who is right?[1] Who is wrong?[2] Which channels are to be trusted,[3] and which are secret sympathisers with the enemy?[4] This week, to help you step through the informational minefield and not lose your grip on those slippery moral gradations, *The Chaser* brings you an Armchair-General's Guide to the War on Terror.

> **Keeping you from un-American thoughts!**

> **I'll help you watch what you say, and what you do, in these difficult times!**

Global international war, particularly war without a defined enemy, can be tough to keep track of! So, to help you find your way through the minefield, we've included this **Cut-Out Ari Fleischer,** for you to place on top of your TV for those moments when you just don't know what to believe!

The Answers
1. *We are.* 2. *They are.*
3. *All of them except SBS.* 4. *SBS.*

ARI FLEISCHER
White House spokesman, Constitutional jurist and bastion of right-thinking people everywhere.

Guide to the War on Terror

WHY IS IT ALL HAPPENING?

Terrorists behave without cause or context, because they are evil, or because they want to take away our freedoms. However, it is important that we retain the freedom of thought and debate that so angers the terrorists. Every now and again, switch across from CNN to some other channel, to ensure that you get to see the available pool footage with a variety of network icons in the upper right-hand corner of the screen, and also to ensure that you hear voice-overs read in American, British and Australian accents. This process is known as 'ensuring balance'.

It is typical for terrorists to work by a tactic known as 'divide and rule'. Firstly, they divide into two groups. The first group stays in a Central Asian country and claims power, establishing a fanatical autocracy. A second group of terrorists then pretend to be persecuted by the first group, in order to gain credibility, then secrete themselves in small boats and starve themselves for weeks on end in order to slip into Australia unnoticed. Luckily, the Australian Government sees through this ruse and ensures that the terrorists, even the dwarf terrorists who dress up as children, get their just desserts!

If you get really stuck (for example, if some of the good guys wear disguises to allow them to pass across the right-hand side of your screen undetected) then use the Cut-Out Ari Fleischer that we have attached (see left).

THE GOOD GUYS

These will be appearing on the left-hand side of your screen. Good guys are identified by the fact that they win in the end.

Colin Powell
US Secretary of State.

George W. Bush
US President and Commander-in-Chief of US Armed Forces.

George Costanza
Played by Jason Alexander in NBC's hit show, *Seinfeld*.

THE BAD GUYS

These will be appearing on the right-hand side of your screen.

Osama bin Laden
Not to be confused with the Osama bin Laden that Casper Weinberger referred to as a 'freedom fighter challenging the evils of Communism in his own land'.

The Taliban
Not to be confused with the Taliban that US President Bill Clinton praised in 1997 for 'reaching across cultural boundaries to join with us in the fight against a common foe – the scourge of the drug industry'. An evil and despicable organisation who seized power after the yoke of Communism was thrown off in Afghanistan by an unrelated organisation of freedom fighters funded by the CIA, confusingly also known as 'The Taliban'. While it is not clear that they are terrorists themselves, they harbour terrorists, with a view to sort of hedging their bets on the whole thing. This will not, as time goes by, prove to be a winning strategy.

Queue Jumpers
The 40 or so trouble-makers in the boat in Nauru seeking to destroy Australia and turn it into an Islamic republic. This threat has now been contained in the secret prison island of Nauru. It isn't clear how Australia came up with the idea of rounding up people who aren't popular and sending them somewhere horrible by boat for life. It is quite likely that in 200 years, Nauru will vote to keep Shane Warne as their Head of State.

The Chaser

Bin Laden lured out of hiding: 'I couldn't miss the Harry Potter premiere'

LONDON, Thursday: Terrorist mastermind Osama bin Laden was apprehended last week at the world premiere of *Harry Potter and the Philosopher's Stone*, ending months of desperate searching by international forces.

The FBI's most wanted man was later seized at the Candy Bar while heatedly telling staff that Allah would 'wreak vengeance' upon them 'with the fire of a thousand suns' after he was charged $6 for a super-sized popcorn.

Prior to his arrest bin Laden, sporting a handsome Armani robe, had appeared at home amongst the glamour set.

'He really turned heads on the red carpet,' enthused one bystander. 'All eyes were on him until Cliff Richard showed up.'

But bin Laden himself was nonplussed by the attendance list. 'It was a bit disappointing really. I was particularly looking forward to meeting Madonna, but apparently she pulled out because of security concerns. Talk about paranoid.'

Yet the notorious extremist remained upbeat about the film itself. 'Two thumbs up!' raved the delighted bin Laden as he was led away by federal agents. 'Sure, it's no *Ishtar*, but there are so few films I can take the kids to these days. The level of gratuitous violence in the media is really worrying for a modern parent. You wouldn't believe the strong images I've been seeing on Al Jazeera lately.'

Discussing the un-ravelling of his plans for world domination, bin Laden was philosophical. 'It was simply a must-see. I missed *The Phantom Menace* because I was

Stars of the new Harry Potter movie, Daniel Radcliffe and Emma Watson, pose with their biggest fan and enemy of the free world, Osama bin Laden

bombing those American embassies and I never heard the end of it from Mullah Mohammed Omar. Besides, it's been a nightmare trying to get new releases under the Taliban.'

The capture of bin Laden is a major breakthrough for the US War on Terror. Without bin Laden, there are now only ten thousand Islamic extremists hell-bent on the destruction of America.

Nevertheless, a Pentagon spokesman was optimistic about some of the Coalition's upcoming military operations. 'There will be plenty more chances to catch terrorists. After all there are at least six more *Harry Potter* sequels this year alone.'

Clerical error sees SES deployed to Afghanistan

SES troops conducting an emu bob across Afghanistan in search of evil

CANBERRA, Tuesday: Staff at the Ministry of Defence yesterday announced that, due to a simple clerical error, it has sent 500 State Emergency Service volunteers to Afghanistan to assist in the ground war.

Satellite pictures have shown long lines of bright orange jumpsuits parachuting from planes deep inside Taliban territory.

However, initial fears for the safety of the SES officers appear to have been misplaced. It was reported early this morning that they had successfully carried out a seek-and-destroy mission on Osama

bin Laden, the leader of the Al-Qaeda terrorist network. 'We were amazed,' said outgoing Defence Minister Peter Reith. 'We didn't know they had that sort of capability.'

Unfortunately, the SES team then rescued bin Laden from under the rubble of his collapsed cave and revived him.

They have spent the hours since searching in vain for a bushfire or a flood in Afghanistan's arid, dry landscape.

Meanwhile, closer to home, members of the Army's elite SAS division rescued a cat from a tree this morning.

Sports Comment
with Harold Parkes
Ed deserves a white hat and a black 'n' white guernsey to complete the set

The young Edward McGuire spent his deformative years in a small weatherboard house next door to the Parkes clan in Albury-Wodonga. The McGuires inhabited the northernmost dwelling in Victoria, the Parkeses the southernmost in NSW, at my steadfast insistence. No son of mine, I declared to the Melburnian lass who would one day become my ex-wife, will be raised and reared on oval-shaped ovals.

I had the boy mow a large rectangle into the backyard twice weekly with white lines marked at ten-metre intervals. I wore loose shorts day and night to impress upon him that his roots lay to the north.

Eddie and the boy routinely joined forces to mount a challenge in the local soapbox derby. The boy built the vehicle and commandeered it. But it was Ed's roles as convenor of the event, handicapper, principal commentator and referee that handed them victory upon victory until they were forced to part ways at interstate competitions and the boy had to settle for a string of silver medallions.

Since that childhood spent on Beach Street, the lad next door has gone from strength to strength. Now some pinko ABC screen jockey has suggested that a man with such passion, pride and entrepreneurial spirit should leave the commentators' dugout when the Magpies are in town. As ludicrous as a nun on Mykonos, we reckon.

Did we learn nothing in Gallipoli?

The commentary position is a coveted one, and requires nothing short of raw emotion and naked ambition. The great Norman May always said that his best work was the result of a couple of carefully arranged electrodes, programmed to come to life when a pair of green and gold Speedos hit the front. The greats have pioneered similar techniques, demonstrating their commitment to the cause and a willingness to put their bodies on the line. Darrell Eastlake, Simon Poidevin, Bill Lawry and Ray Warren will invariably pull up sore after a bout, but soothed with the balm of a job well done.

A heavy wager also injects that all-important urgency into the call. What could Rabs Warren have achieved poolside at the 2000 Olympic Games had he punted his mother's house on Thorpe in the 200 m free? These are the sacrifices a true commentator makes for the game.

Eddie should pull on a white coat and a black 'n' white guernsey, too, and spend a quarter each as President, commentator, white maggot and full forward. If there's a man capable of filling so many roles, Mr Packer tells me this is he.

The Chaser

Melbourne Cup ends: Gambling a destructive social evil again

MELBOURNE, Saturday: Community groups across Australia have reaffirmed their opposition to gambling in the aftermath of the Melbourne Cup, declaring it a 'blight on society.'

'When it comes to gambling, there are no winners,' announced Australian Council Of Social Service spokesperson Carmen Grimble, 'So I was quite chuffed with second place in our office's annual Melbourne Cup Sweep.'

Rebecca Morgan from the Salvation Army agrees. 'People have to realise that there's nothing glamorous about gambling. It's the drinking, fashions and high society that make the Melbourne Cup the highlight of my year.'

'We Salvos find gambling abhorrent in all its forms. And I know the head of our anti-gambling helpline would concur completely if he hadn't resigned after he got lucky with a $10,000 bet on Ethereal.'

Ethereal: downright evil 364 days of the year

ZZ Top: innocent victims of the war on terrorism and the war on beards

No more beards in Kabul: ZZ Top cancels tour

KABUL, Monday: Veteran US rock outfit ZZ Top has been forced to cancel their concert tour of Afghanistan after their signature long beards fell out of favour with the local population.

The hirsute rockers were told last night that local interest in their tour had waned since ludicrously sized beards stopped being compulsory in the nation's capital. The cancellation sounds a death-knell for the band, which has lately relied on Afghanistan as the last remaining market for beard-derived rock.

The bearded rockers were understood to be a big influence on the ruling Taliban, whose prayers and study of the Koran were regularly interspersed with impromptu renditions of 'Legs'.

A Taliban spokesman said the regime strongly related to ZZ Top's misogynist lyrics, backward values and general washed-up status.

Band members were last night apprehended by US troops just south of Kabul, where soldiers carried out a thorough body search to ensure they weren't harbouring terrorist leader Osama bin Laden inside one of their trademark beards.

The Chaser

New Harry Potter Book!

Pottermania is reaching fever pitch in the lead-up to the release of the new Harry Potter movie *Harry Potter and the Philosopher's Stone*. *The Chaser* proudly presents this excerpt of the next sequel in the series, due for release next year.

Harry Potter and the Goblet of Coke

Harry had never been to London before. On the Underground, Hagrid complained loudly that the seats were too small and the trains too slow, not at all like the fast and comfortable service now offered bi-weekly by British Airways™ direct from London to Barbados or with a free Super Stop-Over® in Boston or New York with accommodation in a selection of Premier© and Superior© hotels included for no additional charge. He sipped on his Coke and reflected on all these experiences as the cool brown liquid filled his stomach.

'I don't know how the Muggles manage without magic and the superior sound quality of Sony's new KV-27FS13 27-inch FD Trinitron® WEGA®, with its 3-Line Digital Comb Filter, Matrix Surround™ Sound, and 16:9 Enhanced Mode,' he said, as they climbed a broken-down escalator which led up to a bustling road lined with shops.

After enjoying Coca-Cola™ from the new 600ml Buddy Bottle®, they passed the Barnes and Noble Books and Multimedia Megastore™ and McDonalds' Family Restaurant™, with its range of tasty and nutritious McSnacks®, but nowhere that looked as if it could sell you a magic wand, despite the wide range of quality merchandise offered in the stores they passed. This was just an ordinary street full of extraordinary purchasing opportunities. Could there really be piles of wizard gold buried miles beneath them?

Suddenly Harry craved Coke again. He rushed to the closest store and bought one. It was delicious!

Man reneges on promise to leave the country if Howard wins again

DARLINGHURST, Monday: A local man has decided he won't leave Australia despite the re-election of the Howard Government. Simon McIntyre, 37, an arts administrator, promised repeatedly during the election campaign that he would 'definitely leave Australia if Howard gets back in,' because the country would 'undoubtedly go to the dogs'. But shortly after Saturday's poll result, McIntyre admitted that he in fact had no plans to leave.

McIntyre has a reputation among his colleagues at the Sydney Theatre Company for not following through on promises of this nature. 'He said he definitely wouldn't stay if Robyn Nevin was appointed Artistic Director, but after the announcement was made, guess who suddenly decided he could live with the decision after all?' said one workmate.

McIntyre's admission that he would not be leaving came after his friend Terry Waters quipped that McIntyre 'had better ring up and book his plane ticket'. Waters said he had come to expect this kind of thing from McIntyre. 'He said exactly the same thing before the 1996 election, and again in 1998,' Waters said. 'This habit will backfire one of these days. If Simon ever does really decide to leave the country, I don't think anyone will believe him.'

McIntyre, who will once again not be vacating Australia in the wake of John Howard's election victory

Director's cut of 'Deuce Bigalow Male Gigolo' released

LOS ANGELES, Wednesday: A new director's cut of the Rob Schneider movie *Deuce Bigalow Male Gigolo* was released today. The director, Mike Mitchell, says that the new version, which runs for 242 minutes, captures elements of his vision that were necessarily sacrificed in the original 84-minute theatrical release. The 're-imagining', as Mitchell puts it, completely reinterprets Bigalow's story, focussing on the tragic elements the director believes were sacrificed by Touchstone Pictures' 'unfortunate decision to play for laughs'. 'There are comedic elements to his story, sure, but Deuce's humanity was left entirely on the editing floor,' Mitchell argues. 'The Bigalow story is about much more than just shagging women who are obese or have narcolepsy,' he said. 'It's even about more than shagging women with hilarious detachable limbs.'

Mitchell's work follows in the long tradition of Hollywood directors releasing 'improved', and inevitably longer, versions of their movies, several years later. 'I think of this as my *Apocalypse Now Redux*,' he said. The deleted scenes which are included in the new version include what Mitchell refers to as Deuce's 'epiphany scene', in which Bigalow falls to his knees and cries 'Why? Why? Why?' after realising that despite his large number of sexual conquests, he has yet to find true love. He also added a 25-minute long internal monologue set in a laundromat where Deuce ponders whether he, like the clothes in the washing machine, will ever be clean again. 'I think of it as his equivalent of a Hamlet soliloquy,' Mitchell explained. 'Except in this case, of course, the question is whether to be or not to be a male gigolo.'

Mitchell believes that his director's cut will finally see Deuce Bigalow taking his rightful place in the pantheon of cinema's greatest heroes, alongside Citizen Kane and Lawrence of Arabia. 'Deuce deserves nothing less,' Mitchell says. 'I feel that now, with my masterpiece restored to its full glory, there can be no doubt that Deuce is world cinema's greatest ever male gigolo.'

The Chaser

Howard dreaming of a white Christmas: Border patrol stepped up

SYDNEY, Tuesday: Prime Minister John Howard revealed his Christmas wish list today and admitted that he is still holding out hope that Australia may have a white Christmas.

'Our win at the last election means that there has never been a better atmosphere for a white Christmas,' said Howard.

Experts said that Australia's position in the Southern Hemisphere made this unlikely but the Prime Minister claimed that the proximity to Pacific Islands actually made it more likely.

Howard said that he was dreaming of a white Christmas 'just like the ones I used to know'. He said that he remembered many white Christmases under Robert Menzies and even complimented Arthur Calwell for his White Australian Christmas Policy.

Howard noted that there would be no exceptions to the push for the white Christmas. He confirmed that customs would be stopping and searching Santa after reports that he may be using his sleigh to smuggle refugees into Australia. Santa will also be required to give assurances that he won't be seeking asylum.

Santa Howard: now using Pacific Islands to decide who is naughty and who is nice

The Chaser

Brush with fame: George Harrison (right) with music mega-stars Paul McCartney (third from left) John Lennon (left) and another unidentified member of 1960s boy band 'The Beatles'

Yoko Ono slams latest Beatle death as derivative

LONDON, Tuesday: Yoko Ono, the widow of John Lennon, has criticised former Beatle George Harrison for attempting to cash in on the legacy of John Lennon. Harrison, 58, died this week at his home in Los Angeles, following a brief battle with cancer and a long battle with Yoko Ono.

Ms Ono last night derided Harrison's contribution to The Beatles as minuscule, and slammed his death as derivative of John's. 'George always lacked creative merit,' she said. 'He was possibly the

worst guitarist in the history of the world. Indeed as a musician he was on a par with Linda McCartney'.

For many fans Lennon was the soul of The Beatles, his angry cynical compositions often forming a counterpoint to the 'silly love songs' that Paul McCartney later happily confessed to writing. Others followed Ringo Starr, loved for his idiosyncratic antics, prominent nose and shameless lack of drumming skill. Many fans were also aware of the presence of George Harrison.

After The Beatles split up in

1970, Lennon moved to New York, released two critically acclaimed solo albums, then slumped into nearly a decade of artistic decline, which saw him produce what many critics say was his most uninspiring work. His death saw a return to form, with record sales picking up strongly on the back of a passing that many saw as 'visionary in its finality.'

Speaking at a press conference in London, Ms Ono said, 'Dying was John's thing – the others only really discovered death

because John led the way.

'You just watch. Ringo and Paul won't be far off, trying to cash in on this death thing themselves in a while. Paul's always been jealous of John's ownership of the whole artistic concept of death.'

An earlier dispute between Yoko Ono and the fanatical fans of John Lennon and The Beatles was settled last year, following the payment of an undisclosed sum of money and an agreement by Ono never to sing, perform or record any piece of music in public, ever again.

Artist's impression of what fireworks might look like off the bridge

NYE fireworks tipped to feature Harbour Bridge

SYDNEY, Tuesday: Sources deep inside the Sydney Town Hall are tipping a large fireworks display to be the centrepiece of this year's New Year's Eve celebrations in Sydney. Rumours suggest the spectacle may feature the Sydney Harbour Bridge. But the Sydney City Council has refused to confirm this. 'I want this year to be something special that the people of Sydney will look back on in years to come and remember,' said Sydney Lord Mayor Frank Sartor. 'The surprise will be spoilt if everyone knows what to expect, so you'll just have to wait and see what we've cooked up.'

As the day draws closer, however, Sydneysiders have noticed the presence of workmen atop the Sydney Harbour Bridge and a variety of other elevated points on the city skyline. Legal secretary Chloe Barnard, who works in the CBD's Governor Phillip Tower, reported seeing a number of men in overalls using the lifts over the past week. 'We just don't see much King Gee in here, so they stood out, I guess. Then someone noticed a badge on their uniforms that said Fireworks Unlimited, so word got around that they must be working on the roof.'

The news that the fireworks will involve the Harbour Bridge has disappointed some Sydney residents who had banked on a change in approach. 'I paid top dollar for an apartment with a view over Parramatta's Westfield Plaza because I heard a rumour it would be the main focus of Sydney's New Year's Eve celebrations,' said Vanessa Johnson of Westmead.

The rumours have received additional fuel from a call that several Sydney newspapers and radio stations received early on Monday morning from an anonymous source close to Sartor. 'There are definitely going to be fireworks, lots of them,' the source said. 'I wouldn't even be surprised if the Bridge went up. Seriously.'

Santa starting to question own existence

NORTH POLE, Sunday: Father Christmas is reported to have spent the past few days riddled with self-doubt, questioning for the first time whether he really exists.

The mythical Yuletide character is said to be taking seriously mounting reports that he isn't real. Sources close to the fictional creation say that Santa always believed in himself as a young child, but has developed increasing doubts and scepticism as he's grown older.

'I think he'll take it okay, once he finally accepts it,' said one undisclosed source. 'My real concern is how he'll break it to his elves.'

MIDRIFF TOPS WERE ALL THE RAGE WITH AFGHANI TEENAGERS

Andrew Bliss

The Chaser

Ruddock says space solution not too expensive

The government's new Tampa-Rocket

CANBERRA, Tuesday: Foreign Minister Philip Ruddock has admitted the controversial 'Pacific solution' will soon become untenable after Tuvalu and Fiji refused to accept refugees destined for Australia.

But he vowed to keep refugees from reaching Australia's shore 'at any cost.'

Yesterday Mr Ruddock announced a $450 billion proposal to blast asylum-seekers out of the stratosphere, where they will orbit the globe while their registrations are processed.

The plan will require refugees to do a one-year astronaut course at a NASA installation. There they will learn the basics of living in outer space, skills ranging from surviving on diet pills to pooing without gravity.

Mr Ruddock said that while the cost of the solution may at first seem high, it is what Australians want.

Opposition Leader Simon Crean claimed the policy sent the wrong signal to the world. 'If we go ahead with this project we are sending out a very clear message to refugees, 'Come to Australia and get a free space ride'. This is just the sort of thing that will only encourage these people.'

Independent MP Bob Katter welcomed the plan but said it did not go far enough. 'This is a band-aid solution. Ultimately the government needs to develop a technology that can send refugees back in time so they can kill themselves when they were children. Like in *Terminator*.'

The Australian government has invited its Pacific neighbours to contribute to the scheme, making it clear that the refugee crisis is the entire region's responsibility. So far Palau has pledged twenty rocks and Tuvalu has promised sand and hair.

Super Fly Hip Hop Rapper recommends
The Chaser's Dictionary of Rap™

The Chaser's

DICTIONARY OF RAP™

A Rap-to-English glossary to meet your translation needs!

Understand all your favourite rap artists with this easy-to-use Rap Dictionary™! With patience, soon all you muthaz will be gettin jiggy wit it. This Dictionary™ is also handy for translating **hip hop, trip hop, soul, hip hop soul, underground rap, old school rap, new school rap, metal rap, acid rap, R&B, dirty south rap, east coast rap, west coast rap, alternative hip hop, bass, beats, freestyle, horrorcore, and spiritual rap.** Not suitable for dub.

beat: musical pulse, combination of musical pulses.

bitch: woman, girl. 'I knife that bitch' = 'I injure that woman with the use of a knife.'

chill: pleasant, relaxed. 'This is one chill club' = 'This establishment is pleasant.'

couple: couple of. 'Grab a couple grand' = 'Obtain a couple of thousand dollars.'

cuttin it: spending time; performing rap. 'Cuttin it wit P. Diddy' = 'Performing rap with the artist formerly known as Puff Daddy but now known by the more sensible name P. Diddy.'

da: the. 'Da stuff' = 'The things.'

f/: featuring. All rap releases since 1999 are attributed to one artist featuring another artist. 'Busta Rhymes f/ P. Diddy' = 'Busta Rhymes featuring the artist formerly known as Puff Daddy.' 'Ghostface f/ Raekwon, Slick Rick' = 'Ghostface featuring the artists Raekwon and Slick Rick.'

flows: song lyrics arranged in rhyming patterns and metre so as to be pleasing to the ear. 'Check my flows, they the real shit' =

'Examine my lyrics, as they are excellent.'

freakin: accursed, damned. 'That ain't no freakin beat' = 'That is not an accursed combination of musical pulses.'

fresh: good, high quality.

fuck yo ass: engage in anal intercourse with you.

fuck yo ass up: assault you.

gangsta: [adj.] particularly offensive. 'Gangsta rap' = 'Particularly offensive genre of music characterised by stylised rhymes and gestures.'

gee: woman, girl. 'You my gee, see' = 'You are my woman, understand?'

get jiggy wit it: prepare yourself to acquire such a mood as is conducive to listening to rap music.

hoe: whore, prostitute, loose woman.

homie: male friend, associate.

hoochie: woman, girl. 'Got me a homie and a hoochie' = 'I have both a male and a female companion.'

I'm-a: I am going to, I shall. 'I'm-a kill you, bitch' = 'I am going to terminate your life, woman.'

kool: good, high quality.

mo: more

mutha: [variant of 'mother'] 1. person. 2. motherfucker, muthafucka. pl. muthaz: people.

muthafucka: wretch, fool, scoundrel. pl. muthafuckaz: fools, bad people.

nigga: African American person. 'I ain't wack nigga' = 'I am not an inadequate black American person.' pl. niggaz.

packin a nine: carrying a firearm. 'Crooked cop packin a nine, I fuck yo ass up one mo time' = 'Unscrupulous police officer carrying a firearm, I shall assault you again.'

ph: f. 'Phreakin' = 'Freakin (qv).'

rap: [verb] to speak in stylised rhymes while making emphatic gestures with the hands. [noun] genre of music characterised by stylised rhymes and gestures.

rollin wit: accompanying. 'I'm rollin wit a bitch' = 'I am accompanying a woman.'

shit: nonsense, poor quality thing. 'Don't give me shit' = 'Do not give me that type of bad thing.' Also: the real shit: a fine, excellent thing. 'Don't give me shit, I want the real shit' = 'Do not give me that bad thing, I want a good thing.'

stuff: [coll. noun] things.

they: they are. 'They way kool' = 'They are of very high quality.'

wack: poor, inadequate. 'You wack' = 'You are inadequate in some way.'

wassup: [interr.] how are you. 'Wassup muthaz?' = 'How are you, people?'

wit: with. Also: wid.

yo: 1. your. 2. excuse me. 'Yo! Muthaz!' = 'Excuse me! People!'

z: s. 'Gorillaz' = 'Gorillas.'

Now it's your turn! Using your new knowledge of the colourful language of rap, translate this actual excerpt from the song 'Get 'Em' by Playa Fly featuring Blackout and Lil Terror:

'Enemies chokin' slugs, ain't gotta show me love nigga huh nigga what, ain't playin' nigga thug say what you wanna say, it's Playa posse day and Minnie fuckin' Mae, give us our earned pay as Bill Chill lay, we still love and hate, bump til your heart decay, scared ah me I don't play Blackout bossin' the track, hater callin' ya wack Anna gimme the Mack, y'all ah make it a crack lyrical the attack, blow your heart out ya back broke knots wid Playa Fly, come through wid Gangsta Blac.'

Please send your written translation direct to *The Chaser*. We ourselves can't wait to discover the meaning of these phreakin lyrics! Later muthaz!

Selectors drop Slater from Orange mobile ad

Michael Slater in the famous pageboy-sets-the-table scene from *Macbeth*

SYDNEY, Tuesday: Former test cricketer Michael Slater has been dropped from the Orange mobile phone advertisement, after selectors became concerned about his recent performance.

The selectors explained it was a difficult decision, but said they were left with no option given the poor form Slater has shown all summer on the ad.

Head selector Trevor Hohns said it was apparent 'personal problems' had been distracting Slater from his acting duties.

An angry and disappointed Slater last night took a swipe at the selectors, arguing that his performance had been no worse than any other player's in the advertisement. The former test opener compared his record to that of Mark Waugh, who he

claims has failed successively in his last few campaigns for Ansett and Nizoral.

It's expected Slater will be replaced in the Orange ad by spinner Shane Warne, whose adeptness with mobile phones will lend sorely needed experience to the Australian line-up.

Michael Bevan will be retained for the ad, and will be

used in combination with Warne to provide spin on a lame product that definitely needs it.

Selectors have refused to speculate on whether Slater will be recalled to the ad. It's understood the New South Wales batsman is meeting with Greg Matthews to discuss his possible selection in an Advanced Hair Studio ad for sideburns.

OBITUARY

Winona Ryder

Aspiring shoplifter and actress

1971–2001

The Hollywood retailing community is celebrating today after the death of celebrity thief Winona Ryder. The death is the latest in a series of publicity disasters for Ryder, and has left many critics speculating that her acting career may be over.

Ryder's reputation had hit rock bottom last week after she was arrested for stealing $5,000 worth of clothing from the exclusive Wilshire Boulevard. Ms Ryder's lawyer had dismissed the incident as a 'misunderstanding', arguing that her high-profile client had never had to pay for any clothes since she became famous and had 'just forgotten that you have to'.

But the incident took an even more serious turn when Ryder was charged with 'possessing pharmaceutical drugs without a prescription'. Her pharmacist has also been charged with supplying drugs through a pharmacy.

After a glittering career which saw her attend many Oscar ceremonies, Ryder died in the ignominious surrounding of a Hollywood county jail. Police have refused to speculate on whether Ryder got access to drugs while in prison, although a spokesman for the police admitted that 'in retrospect letting Winona share a cell with Robert Downey Jr was not the best idea'.

Thousands are now mourning the loss of an actor whose career has been described by respected critics as 'extremely lucrative'. Born

Winona Laura Horowitz, the aspiring actor was told at an early age to change her name if she wanted to become famous. Taking this advice to heart, she chose the name Ryder due to her poor spelling, while the name Winona was retained as the result of a clerical error.

Ryder achieved fame at the age of 15 when she starred in her first feature film and quickly moved into the celebrity set. She developed a close friendship with Jennifer Capriati and started going out with fellow actor Johnny Depp at the age of just 17. Ryder met the older Depp while he was doing undercover work at Ryder's high school.

Over the course of her career, Ryder played a number of very challenging roles, in films such as *Age of Innocence* in which she was cast as a young girl who was innocent. In a number of films *(Looking for Richard, Being John Malkovich, Zoolander)* she took on the even more difficult task of playing herself, performing unconvincingly.

Ryder's career went awry in recent years. Her troubles with the law began in 2000 when, after appearing in the intergenerational romance *Autumn in New York,* her co-star Richard Gere was charged with having sex with a minor, merely on the evidence of his on-screen romance with Ryder. (Gere was later acquitted when a jury found the suggestion that

Ryder could fall for Gere too preposterous to support a conviction). The incident put Ryder on a spiral of decline however, which drove her to drink, drugs and working with Ben Stiller. She had tried to find salvation on the stage, but was driven into a deep depression when she could not even secure a naked role in *The Blue Room*.

As expected, the death produced a full scale Hollywood funeral. Hosted by Billy Crystal and attended by some of the big names in the movie industry including Renée Zellweger, Pete Postlethwaite and Arnold Schwarzenegger, the short ceremony was a fitting tribute to the life and career of Winona Ryder and featured a coffin decked with a superb collection of red roses which sources close to the Ryder family insisted had been 'donated' by Roses Only.

HOW TO MAKE CHRISTMAS EGG NOG

1. Ask yourself: do you really want to make Egg Nog?

2. Into a blender pour 4 cups of milk, 4 eggs, 2 tspns of vanilla extract, 3 tspns of sugar, 2 cups of ice cream

3. Blend for 1 minute on high

4. Take one sip and pour rest down drain.

The Chaser

25th January 2002

The party gets under way amid the host's authentic September 11-themed decorations

Host regrets going with September 11 theme for party

MELBOURNE, Sunday: A young Fitzroy woman has admitted that in retrospect she was ill-advised to make 'September 11' the theme of her recent housewarming party. She said that what was intended to be a hip, tongue-in-cheek 'bit of fun' ended up turning her party into a distinctly solemn affair.

'The mood was just really down,' she said. 'People came dressed covered in ash, or clutching a photo of a lost loved one. There was definitely a real negative vibe happening.'

Other guests reportedly turned up carrying boarding passes and box-cutting knives. Another simply came in a small child-size coffin. The host said the morbid atmosphere made it difficult to get a vibrant dance floor going.

'To be fair, I probably should have asked the DJ to play at least one other song besides God Bless America,' she said. 'And it was definitely a mistake to set the smoke machine to the "black smouldering debris" setting.'

The host also noted that some of the people she invited failed to arrive at all, having interpreted September 11 as the date of the party, rather than its theme. 'They actually thanked me for giving them so much notice,' she said. While she was grateful that most of her guests got into the spirit of the terrorist attack theme, she said the gatecrasher who flew a plane into the side of her apartment had taken things way too far.

Volunteer firefighter would have preferred a holiday

Christie and friends unenthusiastically battle the blaze

Christie: resentful

DUBBO, Tuesday: Bill Christie, a volunteer member of the Rural Fire Service, has admitted that he is annoyed at having to give up his Christmas holidays fighting fires hundreds of kilometres from his own home. Christie described the Prime Minister's endorsement of the volunteer spirit as 'total crap'.

The firefighter told reporters that he had mainly joined the RFS to get time off work. 'But to be honest, if they'd said at the start that I could make a choice between fighting fires and taking my annual leave to spend Christmas with the kids, I'd never have signed up,' he said.

Christie says he spent most of December hoping not to get a call from his local RFS commander. 'We kept the phone off the hook as much as possible and I didn't go into town much so that I didn't run in to him there, but one of the bloody kids forgot about the phone and I had to take the call. You don't want to do it, but you can't really say no.' He then spent the next fortnight begrudgingly fighting against various bushfires across NSW, functioning on limited breaks and hardly any sleep.

The firefighter was relieved of his duties on 6 January 'just in bloody time to go back to work on the 7th. My boss told me that he's really proud of what I did, but he didn't say "why don't you have a few days off to relax" or give me my annual leave back. The volunteer spirit just about runs out before it hits the boss's hip pocket'.

The volunteer says he intends to remain in the RFS 'to see if I get any commendations or awards or something like that' but that if he doesn't, he will resign in the upcoming winter.

But not everyone shares the volunteer's perspective. A producer for Channel 9's *A Current Affair* said that the bushfires were a 'great triumph for the Aussie spirit, not to mention making the *Summer Edition* a hell of a lot easier'.

NOW CLASS, BILLY AND SUSIE ARE GOING TO READ YOU THEIR ESSAYS. BILLY'S WRITTEN "WHAT I DID ON MY HOLIDAYS", AND SUSIE'S WRITTEN "THE NIGHT THE MASKED MEN CAME AND KILLED MY DAD."

AaBbCcDdEeFfG.

a Weldon.

Andrew Weldon

The Chaser

Big Day Out tragedy: Young girl survives Ratcat set

AUCKLAND, Friday: Organisers of the Big Day Out music festival have expressed their sorrow to the parents of a teenage girl, who tragically lived through the entire 40-minute set of the washed-up guitar band Ratcat.

Witnesses say the girl had done her best to get crushed in the mosh pit during their performance, but that she was mercilessly left untrampled and forced to endure the simplistic, cartoonish pop from the dated Sydney three-piece.

'It was really awful,' observed one witness. 'I could see the look of terror on her face as they struck up "That Ain't Bad", but there was just nothing I could do. I just felt so powerless as I stood by and watched her live.'

The event's organisers have defended their decision to let the band continue playing in the face of such tragic survival. They said the girl's endurance was 'completely unforeseeable', but agreed they would review security measures to make it easier for music fans to die during lame acts in the future.

It's the second Big Day Out tragedy in successive years, following last year's horrific incident when all but one fortunate girl was subjected to a typically brash, unmusical set by Limp Bizkit.

Devastated

Mugabe nears victory of black oppressors over white oppressors

HARARE, Thursday: In a key policy speech, Zimbabwe's 77-year-old bewitched President, Robert Mugabe, made a strong statement of his government's achievements and vision in the lead-up to securing the continuation of his rule by a token election. The President condemned the current political violence, which he said should be restricted to intimidation in the fortnight preceding election day.

'We have obliterated the inequitable property divisions which scarred our country,' Mr Mugabe said. 'The whities have gone home, and our hyper-inflation strategy has redistributed the savings of the rich.' The President also praised his party's efforts in 'eliminating the last traces of Western constitutionalism, which runs contrary to the African values of personalist dictatorship and militarism.'

'Zimbabweans want minority government based on cronyism, not race; they want to be oppressed by their own,' he said.

Mr Mugabe later boasted that his new Internal Security Act 'should utterly abolish journalism, and frustrate the neo-imperialist agenda of the Manchester *Guardian* and its agents.'

Mugabe celebrates his coming victory over whities, the spirit realm, and people who say that twin-tone caps look stupid

Mr Mugabe outlined his new vision for his country, based on the Congo, where thousands of Zimbabwean troops have been stationed for several years. Describing the anarchic former Belgian colony as 'a giddy whirlpool of fun', Mr Mugabe suggested that Zimbabwe will consider becoming 'the second blind eye of Africa', abolishing its currency, judiciary, police force, parliaments and borders. 'For the first time in nearly three hundred years,' he said, 'ghosts and other spirit beings would make public policy, and implement it through mob violence.'

Golf course deluged with balls the size of hail stones

US liberates Afghan women: Kabul's first Hooters opens

KABUL, Monday: Following the demise of the backward Taliban regime, Hooters has finally opened an outlet on Kabul's main street of Jade Maiwand. The chain now proudly offers Afghan women the kind of modern, liberated way of life that Westerners take for granted by recruiting them to become 'Hooters Girls'.

'We liberated Afghanistan from Taliban control, and now Hooters is liberating Afghan women too,' explained the restaurant's manager, Jay Smythe. 'Instead of being forced to stay at home and look after their menfolk, Afghan women can become Hooters Girls and get paid for doing the same thing.'

'The Taliban also forced women to wear those highly degrading, restrictive "burqua" clothes,' he pointed out. 'But thanks to us, they are now free to wear the world-famous Hooters low-cut tank-top and sexy orange shorts!'

Smythe says that parent company Hooters of America Inc. is willing to sacrifice short-term profitability in the interests of rebuilding Afghanistan. 'Hooters of Kabul is about more than just dollars – as a company that employs only females in our dining area, we're all about empowering the women of Afghanistan by offering them a great job,' he said. 'It's part of the Hooters commitment to a better world.'

The chance to work in Hooters is just one of the ways in which Westernisation has improved the lot of women in the new Afghanistan. But it is still very early days.

'The Taliban oppression of women has been so substantial that it will take decades to undo – it's almost as if they've been brainwashed into their backward, unemancipated lifestyle,' said the editor of a new local version of *Ralph* magazine, *Abdul*. 'As a result, we're having enormous trouble finding local girls who feel free enough to pose topless.'

New Hooters Girl Fatima still isn't entirely comfortable with abandoning some parts of the Taliban's dress code

OBITUARY

Kerry Jones

Monarchist, quasi-politician and Moran

c1857–2002

Truly a Moran

The Queen of the Australian Anti-Republic movement has departed this earth to join the great Constitutional Monarchy in the sky after apparently taking her own life. The death of Kerry Jones, eldest child of the nursing home magnate Doug Moran and noted feminist Greta Moran, is the latest in a succession of tragedies for the Moran family. As they move into grieving mode once again, it is expected that several factions of the Moran family will attend a very public memorial service for Ms Jones this Friday.

The circumstances of Ms Jones' death remain a mystery, but sources close to the family say they are expecting to discover a 'rather long exit note' from Ms Jones. Lawyers for the estate of Ms Jones have released a statement saying they will 'wait until we get to the Supreme Court before speculating about the real reasons for Ms Jones' death'.

Ms Jones is the second of the Moran children to die before their time, after younger brother Brendan committed suicide in 1995 in an attempt to provide for his wife Kristina. After the last death, rather than opting for an intensive course of therapy the family decided upon a vicious and protracted suite of litigation to confront their grief. It is expected the family will adopt a similar course in response to Ms Jones' untimely death.

Kerry Moran was born in the late 1950s, although the precise year of her birth is unknown as the family did not observe birthdays. In an affidavit in support of her father in the 1980s, Ms Jones described her child-hood growing up with Doug and Greta as 'idyllic' and 'wonderful'.

The young Kerry's relationship with her parents declined later, however, when she decided to marry accountant Michael

TIMELINE

How the World Changed Forever

September 9
World pretty samey

September 10
World still samey

Jones. Patriarch Doug did not approve of the union, expressing concern to close associates that a marriage to an accountant might enable Kerry to get her hands on some of the family money. After a falling out, Kerry and her husband moved to Wagga where Kerry tried to forge her own career as a kindergarten teacher, bringing the distinctive Moran style of caring to her young charges.

But the appeal of independent achievement soon faded and Ms Jones returned to the fold, taking up a six figure salary to sit on the board of the Moran Foundation for Older People which had been created by Doug and Greta to provide their aging children with 'continuing day care'. Unsatisfied with the socially progressive nature of her work with the Foundation, Ms Jones decided to embark on a career

in Liberal politics. Jones' strategy essentially involved having her father buy her pre-selection in a safe Liberal seat in the NSW State Parliament, but the surprisingly high price of such a seat (given their rarity at the time) and an unprecedented resort to merit criteria resulted in Ms Jones being excluded.

But just as it looked as if Jones' career in public life was doomed, she discovered a niche for herself within Australians for a Constitutional Monarchy (ACM), the flagship organisation for the fight against the move for Australia to become a republic. Jones had a meteoric rise within the organisation, thanks in part to a significant injection of funds into ACM from the family, but mainly the fact that the impressive host of high profile supporters of the monarchist cause involved in ACM

(including Justice Michael Kirby, Sir Harry Gibbs and Dame Leonie Kramer) had better things to do.

The anti-republic campaign turned out perfectly for Jones, who derided the arguments in favour of a republic with glib and often nonsensical retorts, a style she developed after close study of the public statements of Pauline Hanson and Sir Joh Bjelke-Petersen. The referendum was ultimately successful for the anti-republican cause, without Jones having to resort to the infamous Plan M under which all nursing home residents would have been threatened with eviction if they did not vote 'No'.

After the success of the referendum, Jones charac-teristically failed to convert her profile into another useful public role. Despite more overtures to the Liberal Party, she returned to her work with the Foundation

until late 2001, when her father moved to oust her from her position on the Board. Jones prepared herself, and several major law firms, for a protracted battle with her father, who she described as 'eccentric and irrational', an expression which earned her a nomination for Australian Euphemism of the Year.

As the battle with her father developed, Ms Jones reportedly became more and more dispirited. It is understood she spent a lot of time with Kristina Moran and told friends that she 'felt closer and closer to Brendan'. Ms Jones tried to reconcile with her father, seeking to make him change for the better, but she was unable to argue the case effectively. The meeting ended with Mr Moran telling his daughter to 'do the right thing by the family'. She has not been seen since.

September 11, 8.40 a.m.
World starts to change

September 11, 8.42 a.m.
World noticeably different

September 11, 10.50 a.m.
World changed forever

chase up ◆ HARASSMENT OF THE RICH AND FAMOUS ◆

The reshuffle in the top ranks of PBL makes it pretty clear Kerry is about to die. So *The Chaser* wrote Kerry a note to read on his death bed.

Kerry Packer
c/- Consolidated Press Holdings
Fax: (02) 9267 2150

Dear Kerry,

I noticed that you're not looking too well, and, quite frankly, we're all pretty sure that you're about to die.

Before you do, I was wondering whether you've been through all your options about your inheritance? I know people must come up to you all the time and ask to be put on your will, but we thought we'd throw our hat in the ring anyway.

Let's face it: Jamie's going to blow your money. Look at him. He's not even interested in media assets (although I understand he is interested in another type of assets, if you get my meaning). No matter how many John Alexanders you put between him and the money, it's going to start disappearing the moment the ink dries on your death certificate.

If you sign over all your assets to The Chaser then you can rest assured that at least your legacy of proudly independent Australian media will live on.

Regards,

Charles Firth
Co-Editor
The Chaser

P.S. You should sign them over before you die to avoid certain tax liabilities – we know how much you hate paying them.

www.chaser.com.au
Phone: (02) 9380 5051 Fax: (02) 9356 8591

Western viewers claim Asian soccer stadiums all look the same

Shake-up at Nine as Packer looks for new faces, kidneys

SYDNEY, Tuesday: Channel Nine boss Kerry Packer has ordered a complete re-structure of the station's management, after becoming aware that many of his old executive team had incompatible organs.

Among the first to go was the station's chief executive David Leckie, who maintained Channel Nine's position as the top-rating network for more than ten years, before redesigning a brand new ratings system which placed the network sixth.

Mr Packer denied Leckie's sacking had anything to do with the fact the station was now rating lower than Channel 31. He said Leckie's departure was purely about letting some new blood into the network, preferably of Packer's blood type.

'The fact of the matter is,' elaborated Mr Packer, 'that Leckie just no longer had the heart for this business. More specifically, he no longer had a heart for me.'

Among several new programming changes, Mr Packer has asked that all patients on the hospital show *RPA* now be forced to surrender their kidneys as a matter of course.

He's also told the incoming management team that the station needs fresh new talent, which might explain why Nine recently re-signed Don Burke and Eddie McGuire for 20 more years each.

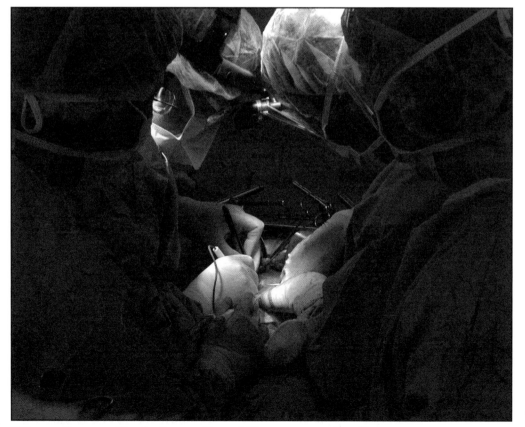

PBL executives recruiting for the new Channel Nine management positions

EMAIL PUNCTUATED

AN EPOCH-SHATTERING report has come through that Sydney office worker Mr Philip Pryor yesterday sent one of his friends an email that was fully punctuated.

ASIO is investigating the case, and there is an unconfirmed suggestion that the email in question was also spaced correctly, with appropriate paragraph breaks.

Our inside sources have roughly estimated the full text of the email:

Hi there Jean,
The weekend's all set!
It's been hectic here at work, especially with all our clients' Christmas arrangements, but now the end is in sight. Would you be able to bring along a salad to the barbecue?
If it's too much trouble, let me know. (I mean that - don't go and stress over it!)
Of course I invited Damian, and he said, 'I'll think it over.'
See you soon,
Philip.

Our experts have attempted to decipher the bizarrely coherent email, and they arrived at the following translation into regular email-English:

hi there jean th weekends all set, its been hectic here@work es pcially w- all our cLients xmas arrangements
But now th ends sight.. Wd u b able 2 brng along salad 2 t bbQ if 2 much trouble let know i mean that don t
go _stress re it

of course i invite d. he said ill think it over cu soon p.

The Chaser

NSW introduces truth-in-breaking-up legislation

SYDNEY, Thursday: Following his successful truth-in-sentencing legislation, NSW Premier Bob Carr will introduce truth-in-breaking-up legislation. 'It's a natural progression – both laws are to make people say what they actually mean,' he said. The Premier believes the legislation must be passed urgently to avoid the widespread use of the violent American method of discovering the truth underlying a break-up, which involves a confession on the *Jerry Springer Show*.

Carr says that everyone has the right to fair dealing and honesty from lovers, just as they do from businesses. 'Hypothetically, if someone said they were breaking up with me because I was the Premier and married and they didn't want the press to find out, but the real reason was because they'd dumped me for the Treasurer, I'd definitely have the right to know,' he argued. 'Hypothetically.'

The move follows a recent campaign by the ACCC to stamp out the false advertising of relationship status by people in bars. According to Professor Allan Fels, many people who describe themselves as single when chatting up a prospective partner are engaging in deceptive or misleading conduct. The Commission is now insisting that singles fully disclose their status as 'single but still sleeping with my ex-boyfriend a few nights a week' or 'single, but not through my choice so much as the restraining order'.

Nothing to hide: Bob Carr and someone else

The truth-in-breaking-up laws in practice

OLD LIE	NEW TRUTH
It's definitely not you, it's me	It's definitely not me, it's you
There isn't anyone else	There isn't anyone else, but God I wish there was
I swear there's not another woman	There is another man
I just need some space	This relationship is over
This just isn't the right time	You just aren't the right person
We can still be friends	I never want to see you again
I just need to get my head straight	I just need to sleep around
You're the one for me, I'm just not ready to commit yet	I want to keep you around in case I can't find anyone better to marry
Yes, we can go out on Saturday night, but just as friends	I want to sleep with you without you thinking we're back together
I want to be able to see other people while I'm away	I want to be able to break up with you when I get back

ILLEGAL IMMIGRANT HIDEOUT- BONDI, N.S.W

THANK CHRIST WE ESCAPED all that REPRESSION...

THE BENNY HILL SHOW

Fiona Katauskas

The Chaser

Dad guy from 'Hey Dad!' finally gets another acting job

Hey Dad! was the longest-running sitcom ever made and it hasn't aged a bit

SYDNEY, Tuesday: middle-aged Australian actor Robert Hughes, who played the role of architect and father Martin Kelly in the long-running television program *Hey Dad!*, has obtained his first acting role after the series ended its ten-year run in 1994. Hughes admits the search for work after *Hey Dad!* has been very difficult.

'As if sharing a name with the nation's most internationally famous prick wasn't bad enough', said Hughes, 'I think it's fair to say that being Martin Kelly for so long hasn't helped me achieve the diversity I would have liked in my acting career.'

Apart from a short stint in an ill-fated pantomime version of *Hey Dad!* that opened off London's West End in 1995, Hughes has auditioned for over 700 roles since 1994 without success. 'I've had more job offers from architecture firms actually,' Hughes admitted.

'I turned up for all manner of roles, but the feedback was always the same. "My kids loved your show", they'd say, "but we just can't see Martin Kelly as King Lear being taken seriously".' Hughes says he understands what they were saying, but that he wishes his performances could be judged on their merits. 'I'll admit that my Lear was unconventional, but I think the audience would really have gone for the Fool being played by that hair-brained funster, Betty Brainbuster.'

In the early days Hughes could survive on the strength of royalties from repeats of *Hey Dad!*, but the money soon dried up. 'The money pretty well dried up after '96,' said former Executive Producer Gary Reilly. 'And the '99 digitally remastered DVD release was a complete disaster.'

Hughes acknowledges that his inability to find work in his chosen profession caused him to suffer deep depression in the late 1990s. But things are now looking up. Hughes has secured a role in a new David Williamson comedy of manners about a middle-aged actor who has fallen on hard times. And Hughes is looking on the bright side. 'It was a long time between drinks, but at least I can say that I was the first one in the cast to get another job'.

Celebrity advice

With special guest Dr John Gray

Author of *Men are from Mars, Women are from Venus*

Q: I am married to a man who refuses to help out around the home, even though we both work full time. How can I get him to do his share without alienating him?

A: **Many people don't realise this but at about six weeks *in utero*, a foetus's gender is determined, sealing a portion of the fate of every one of us. Armed with this understanding, you will come to see your relationship in an entirely new light. Rather than labeling your husband as 'bad' for 'not doing his share', you will come to see that he just approaches the idea of sharing differently. Rather than criticising him, and expecting him to be just like you, respect and even rejoice in your differences. With this new attitude, you may just find yourself enjoying rather than resenting the time you spend cleaning the toilet or defrosting the freezer.**

Q: I am a 45-year-old man currently dating a 38-year-old woman with two children aged 6 and 8. It seems that, because the kids are always around, we rarely have time for one-on-one intimacy. Is there a tactful way to address this problem?

A: **Many millennia ago, when we were all foetuses living in caves and hunting and gathering, our synapses and nerve centres were being formed, in an evolutionary process much like we see today. The question then is: what are the implications of our prehistoric yearnings and instincts for contemporary, and often complex relationships? For some of us, sectors of our brains have developed in such a way that we exhibit a talent for merchandising, although not necessarily for evolutionary biology. For others, development occurs in such a way that the 'purchasing' and 'gullibility' functions are paramount. You fit into the latter category and may benefit from my book *Mars and Venus Starting Over*.**

8th February 2002

CENSORSHIP LEGISLATION OUTSTANDING!

Canberra, Friday: The community and media have reacted with enthusiasm to the government's proposed harsh and very fair penalties for espionage and the leaking of government documents.

The Civil Liberties Council has welcomed the legislation claiming it will prevent destabilising journalism which uncovers nothing, because there is no government impropriety.

'This legislation would have meant that the Peter Reith phonecard public triumph would never have been misrepresented by the press,' said Cameron Arsehole of the NSW Council for Civil Liberties.

The proposed legislation led to some happy reactions from journalists.

Political commentator Alan Ramsay said that Attorney-General Daryl

Daryl Williams: world's greatest wit

A public rally to celebrate the government's new espionage legislation

Williams was 'the world's greatest wit'.

'If he thinks he can implement this toast to the Australian people's rights then he's got another easy re-election coming', Ramsay slurred.

The legislation comes after the government has been enhanced by revelations that their members have been involved in sporting and travel anecdotes.

The laws will not even allow leaks that are in the public interest, including news that John Howard and his secretary, Barbara, have been having a professional relationship involving mutual admiration.

Rafter performs some of his new official duties as Bermudan of the Year

Rafter named Bermudan of the Year for tax purposes

BERMUDA, Tuesday: The newly announced Australian of the Year, former tennis player Pat Rafter, was also named Bermudan of the Year today in a simple ceremony held in Bermuda's Parliament. In accepting the award, Rafter said while he was proud to be an Australian citizen and Australian of the Year, he was even more proud of Bermuda because of its more enlightened approach to many areas of public policy, particularly income tax rates.

Rafter said the award was flattering because of his great love for Bermuda and its people, but would also have the additional benefit of clarifying his residency status with the Australian Taxation Office. 'Some cynical people in the ATO might think that just because I'm being honoured as a pre-eminent Australian and will spend most of the year travelling around the country to preside at various official ceremonies, I've somehow become an Australian resident for tax purposes.' Rafter clarified that his 'close emotional ties' with his adopted homeland of Bermuda make that impossible.

As Bermudan of the Year, Rafter says he is planning to spend 'at least' the 30 days on the island required to qualify as a resident for taxation purposes under Bermudan law. Though some critics have described Rafter's Bermudan residency as a 'tax dodge', Rafter insists it is based on a strong desire to contribute to Bermudan society. 'Tax is how individuals contribute to the society they live in, and it's a means of contributing to the common good. My fellow Bermudans and I have chosen, for ethical reasons, to contribute to a progressive society that has opted to abolish income tax,' he explained.

Rafter will also continue his role with the phone company 1800-REVERSE despite attracting heavy criticism from the Australia Day Council for his insistence on reversing the charges when calling to accept the Australian of the Year award.

This year, Rafter will also be launching his own phone service, 1800-TAX-AVERSE.

Bermuda's Premier, Jennifer Smith, says that Australians who have criticised Rafter's motives in living in Bermuda don't know their own luck. 'You should appreciate Rafter as much as we do,' she said. 'Do you have any idea how much we would have liked him to play for our Davis Cup team?'

Smith says she is extremely gratified that he continues to reside in Bermuda despite being made Australian of the Year. 'We're very proud of Pat. So proud, in fact, that we were only too happy to name him Bermudan of the Year when he asked.'

Anthony Robbins helps refugees turn that frown upside down

WOOMERA, Sunday: The Department of Immigration and Multicultural Affairs and Motivator and Life Coach Anthony Robbins have established a Robbins Results Coaching Partnership to ease depression and reduce incidents of self-harm among residents of Australia's immigration detention centres.

'During the 6-week program we have developed, we will ask asylum seekers "What is it you can do to pursue the life you desire and deserve?" and challenge them to find ways they can turn their lives around, today,' says Robbins. 'In particular, we will challenge the asylum seekers to consider whether they will continue to allow fear, depression and anger to run their lives, or whether they will embrace faith, determination, love and gratitude. They clearly have the choice'.

Re-evaluating the asylum

Robbins outside the renamed 'Woomera Opportunity Centre'

seekers' approach to time management is key to turning around their attitudes, and in turn, their life. As one Division Head of DIMA notes 'Currently, the average asylum seeker spends 2.4 hours per day on negative self-talk, 4.3 hours per day sitting around and 2.3 hours

per day contemplating or carrying out self-harm. As Anthony points out, that time could be much better spent making business contacts, maximising business exposure or maintaining intimate relationships in simple ways like sending a bunch of flowers or an

affectionate note.' Other components of the 6-week course include 'Wealth Mastery', 'Leadership Academy' and 'Unleash the Power Within'. Attendees will be offered a 10% discount on Anthony Robbins multimedia products including RPM software and planners.

Asians relieved by Arab victimisation

Anti-Arab racism allows Asians to rebuild their reputations

CHERRYBROOK, Saturday: Asian community leaders have expressed relief at the growing vilification of Middle Eastern immigrants. Recent polls have shown that the Middle Eastern community have taken over the Asian community as the most vilified ethnic group in Australia.

'General malaise' towards Asians was down 6.5% for the last quarter of 2001, while 'blind hatred' slipped by a record 6.3%.

'We haven't been less hated since the death of Victor Chang,' said a spokesperson for the Asian community.

In contrast, 23.4% more Australians agreed strongly or very strongly with the statement that 'Muslims and Arabs are the scourge of the earth and the single greatest threat to civilised society' compared with the same period in 2000.

'The worst they can say about us is that we take all the spots in selective schools which should go to Aussie kids,' commented Chinese community leader Mr Henry Wong at Friday's Ethnic Leaders Summit. 'That just doesn't seem as bad as being a threat to global democracy and stability.'

'I guess we would have preferred to have been less vilified due to a newfound understanding for our community rather than because of the ignorant victimisation of another race,' said Mr Wong. 'But you take what you can get.'

Coffee-hater celebrates opening of new Starbucks store

ST KILDA, Saturday: Jill Connor today celebrated the opening of a new Starbucks store in her home suburb of St Kilda.

'I have always hated the taste of coffee, so it's great that I can now get a coffee without any taste,' said Connor.

Connor initially ventured into the Starbucks store because she had heard that there were several alternatives for people who did not like coffee, such as 'Caramel Apple Cider' and 'Tazoberry'.

'In the end I settled on some of their other coffee alternatives such as their "Cappuccino" and their "Caffé Latte",' said Connor.

Another customer, Terry McGraw of Brighton, said he hadn't realised there were so many different types of iced coffee beverages in the world, let alone at the one coffee outlet. 'They've got Iced White Chocolate Mocha, Iced Caramel Macchiato, and even Iced Tazo Chai,' he said. 'Sure, they all sound completely disgusting,' he added, 'but you've got to give them points for variety.'

Several other customers at the Starbucks opening were also impressed by the large size of the store's beverages.

'I just bought myself one of their Grande coffees and it is just great,' said Wendy Jensen, of Carlton. 'Too many of the cafes around here totally stinge on the water, which I find really adds flavour to the coffee.'

The new store as it most often appears: without customers

Howard to hold fresh talks with Megawati's answering machine

JAKARTA, Thursday: Prime Minister John Howard has announced plans to visit Indonesia, where he's scheduled to hold important new talks with President Megawati's voicemail service.

In what several regional analysts are touting to be landmark discussions, Mr Howard will canvass a wide range of issues with several of Indonesia's top-level answering machines.

The official four-day visit will begin with a dinner in the Presidential palace, hastily vacated on the eve of Howard's arrival. The following morning the Prime Minister will meet with Megawati's personal secretary, who will present him with a traditional Indonesian memo explaining that the President is out.

Mr Howard is then scheduled to engage in key diplomatic talks with a number of high-ranking telephonists, who will each put him on hold. He's also expected to attend a number of important round table discussions with a government receptionist who will apologise that no-one else could attend.

The Prime Minister has stressed the importance of maintaining a dialogue with Indonesia, and says he hopes the visit will strengthen his relationship with the country's switchboard operators.

Howard and his dialogue partner, the Panasonic KX-TM150B

EXCLUSIVE TRANSCRIPT

Megawati's answering machine message

'Hi, you've phoned Megawati. I'm not in right now, but if you leave your name and number after the beep, I'll endeavour never to get back to you. If you're ringing to suggest I should crack down on people smuggling, press one. If you'd like me to pull the military out of Irian Jaya or Aceh, press two. Or if you wish to be put through to me directly, then stop telling me how I should run my country.'

Arthur Andersen's Buenos Aires principal outside the Parliament whose work he enthusiastically, if unthinkingly, endorses

Arthur Andersen signs off on Argentina economy

BUENOS AIRES, Tuesday: The turbulent economy of Argentina is reportedly in good shape, according to expert accountants from the international accounting firm Arthur Andersen.

Two senior Andersen auditors yesterday signed off on the country's finances, after a cursory look at the Treasury's books. They assured the Argentine government that the peso was one of the healthiest currencies in the world, and that the country had no monetary worries in the foreseeable future.

Andersen yesterday issued a statement, rejecting accusations that the conduct of its auditors had been anything other than proper. This statement was later shredded by a senior executive. The statement denied suggestions that Andersen's close links to Argentina had pressured them to overlook several glaring budget anomalies, such as the country's all-time record debt and the devaluation of the currency to zero.

The company also denied that its auditors had any improper relationships with Argentinean officials. 'That's absolute nonsense,' insisted chief auditor Senor Pedro Gonzalez during a private dinner with the country's President. The auditor was later observed at the same dinner shredding lettuce out the back.

Financial commentators believe Andersen's international reputation is now on the line, following their similarly controversial role in the collapse of US energy giant Enron and the Australian insurance firm HIH. New evidence also reveals that the company agreed to sign off on the world economy shortly before the Great Depression in the 1930s.

If the company's accountancy arm collapses, it's expected the board will try to reposition Andersen as a specialist waste management and disposal service, providing unparalleled expertise in the removal of sensitive documents.

The firm has reportedly put so much incriminating material through its shredder that a recent ticker-tape parade in Houston had to be redirected away from Andersen's offices, for fear that the downpour would completely bury the marchers.

The Chaser

OBITUARY
Stephen Mayne

Self promoter
1965–2002

Mayne covers own funeral

The serious journalism community is unaffected today after the shock death of crikey.com.au proprietor Stephen Mayne. Mayne is the most prominent person to date to have died in 2002, due to the fact that no-one really famous has passed away this year as well as the amount of self-promotion that Mayne put into his demise. The effects of Mayne's death are already being felt with a marked increase in traffic on Crikey's website already recorded.

Mayne was pronounced dead at 3:59 on Wednesday 6 February 2002 after he was executed by lethal injection in accordance with Commonwealth law (full details – including a leaked snuff video of the execution are available at www.crikey.com.au). Mayne had been convicted by a military tribunal in a secret trial only days earlier after he was arrested for breaching the federal government's new laws against leaking government documents without authorisation. The laws were passed by the Senate just last week soon after the government passed the Minor Party (Consequences of Blocking Government Agenda) Bill 2002.

Mayne's lawyer reacted to the execution saying he had not been aware of Mayne's arrest and was devastated because the journalist had not paid his bills.

Mayne's demise came

after he published leaked Commonwealth documents criticising the new anti-leaking laws. Phillip Ruddock – given ministerial responsibility for the new laws because of his strong track record in defending contemptible policy – said the public servants involved 'have also been dealt with'. At the military hearing, he ran his own defence which was based primarily on the fact that he had posted the Alan Jones blooper tape on the internet some hours after everyone in the country had received it by email (for full details including the blooper tape, visit www.crikey.com.au).

The death brings to an end a career. Mayne first achieved notoriety in 1999 as the creator of the website www.jeffed.com which wittily presented lunatic right wing views as if they had been implemented as government policy. Mayne got the idea for the site while

working for Jeff Kennett, implementing lunatic right wing views as government policy. (For full details including accounts of everything that Mayne has ever done, visit www.crikey.com.au) . Prior to that, Mayne had worked for a succession of Australian newspapers compiling an impressively large number of former work colleagues. This network of associates was useful to Mayne when he set up his own media outlet (www.crikey.com.au), giving him a huge list of possible contacts who had to invent reasons for not returning his calls.

Mayne achieved a high profile in his last few years through Crikey (that's www.crikey.com.au) and his shareholder activism. Mayne started buying shares in publicly listed companies so that he could harangue board members after a discussion with serial pest Peter Hore. In

the years that followed, Mayne annoyed many directors, giving vicarious pleasure to Crikey's small readership (which consisted mainly of plaintiff defamation lawyers) without achieving any changes in corporate policy.

Over time, however, Crikey developed a steady readership of media and politics insiders who enjoyed it when the groundless rumours they started were published and then retracted when Mayne got around to checking his facts. Crikey was also the subject of much speculation over the identity of its Liberal insider columnist who wrote under the pseudonym 'Hillary Bray'. For a time it was thought that Bray was an alter-ego for Mayne, but this theory was dismissed on the ground that Bray's quick wit and sharp prose could not possibly have been generated by Mayne (by the way, for a complete archive of Hillary Bray, visit www.crikey.com.au).

News of Mayne's death was slow to spread through media circles after Crikey published an article confirming that Mayne was alive and had been acquitted, a story which it was forced to retract. When the news finally spread, the head of the Australian Journalists' Association released a statement mourning Mayne's loss. 'While a victory for the reputation of our profession, Stephen's untimely death is still a great loss. The anti-leaking laws are an affront to our civil liberties, especially when combined with the death penalty. The laws are likely to have an intolerable impact on Australian journalists, although we can live with it in this case.'

Celebrity cooking advice™
With your guest host:
COLONEL HARLAND SANDERS

Howdy y'all, and welcome to mah finger-lickin' chicken-cookin' column!

I sure have come a long way from owning my own plantation in Kentucky.

Why, nowadays I'm a chatterin' caricature who dances about and spruiks away jest as rootin'-tootin' as you please at the slightest whim of the very same fried chicken restaurant I once created and pioneered!

I sure been hornswoggled! Heh heh heh!

Now, here's one of my favourite recipes – in fact, it's my Original Recipe Kentucky Fried Chicken that nobody knows how to make on account of how it's got eleven secret herbs and spices, jest as secret as they come.

Finally, *The Chaser* reveals exactly how I make this tastebud-tinglin' toe-tappin' testicle-tweakin' treat on two legs! Except for the secret bit.

ALRIGHT, Y'ALL – listen up!

Here's how to make you that finger-lickin' rectum-kickin' mother-chicken that you're cravin'!

Go to a building excavation site.

Pour the oils and fats and salt into the gigantic hole in the ground, and mix together using a Bobcat earth mover.

Murder the chickens.

Pitch the chickens into that tasty batter. Be careful not to burst the cyst on the sick one! Ain't no lucky customer'll start no urban legend unless they chomp down on a plump, juicy bubo now, will they?

Heh heh heh!

Oh – almost forgot! Be sure to firmly wedge the severed finger in the breast of another one of those chickens.

Stir the chickens around in the excavation site with your earth mover. Then fetch 'em out, ten at a time, with the scoop.

Coat them chickens with a good dose of the eleven secret herbs and spices. Now get ready, this is a historical moment, I'm going to tell you what the secret herbs and spices are. They are – are you ready for this? This is being revealed at immense legal risk. This is an epoch-teetering instant. I don't want to build it up. The secret herbs and spices are: MSG, rock salt, brine salt, onion salt, chicken salt, seasoning salt, pork salt, beef salt, smelling salt, non-sodium salt substitute, and parsley.

Oh, sweet bejesus and Jeeeehosephat!!
Jack-a-mo-fee-nah-nay!
I accidentally done gone let out mah secret herbs and spices!
Dagnappit and yippee-i-oh-cai-ay!

What an authentic little television Southerner!

And next issue, we'll be cooking with celebrity chef The Sultan of Brunei.

KFC'S ORIGINAL RECIPE CHICKEN

Serves 250

100 chickens, one with a cyst
1 megalitre vegetable oil
1 megalitre peanut oil
1 megalitre olive oil
1 megalitre sunflower oil
1 megalitre canola oil
1 megalitre cottonseed oil
1 megalitre rapeseed oil
1 megalitre cod liver oil
1 megalitre engine oil

Now, we don't want it to end up too dry, so we add:
1 tonne butter
1 tonne lard
1.5 tonnes shortening
1 tonne ghee
1 employee's index finger, cleanly severed
Last year's combined produce of salt from China, Germany and India
Eleven herbs/spices, secret

38

Celebrity advice

With special guest Bettina Arndt

Q: I recently separated from my husband, after a turbulent and often violent 12-year marriage. I am now seeking to regain control of my life but I'm not quite sure how, I need suggestions for ways to move on and up.

A: **Before you consider leaving your violent marriage, there are a few factors you should consider: (1) Are you morally comfortable with the fact your children's educational opportunities will suffer, leaving them 26% less likely to attain post-tertiary educational qualifications? (2) Have you considered the real reason you are thinking of ending the relationship? Could it possibly be a selfish attempt to deprive your husband of contact with his children in order to punish him for what you perceive as his 'failings' and raise your children in a female-dominated environment where they learn to view masculinity as a negative characteristic? Think carefully.**

Q: I am a busy single mum with two active boys aged 5 and 7 who is seeking some creative ideas for tasty and nutritious treats for my boys' school lunches. Any ideas?

A: **The best thing you can do for your children's nutrition is to marry their father. It is well known that children born into a stable and committed marriage have higher iron levels and rank higher on tests of agility and flexibility than the bastard children of single mothers like you. Although marriage may have been far from your mind when you conceived your children, it is now time for you to consider their welfare rather than your selfish desire to create tasty and nutritious snacks with which to stuff their lunch boxes.**

Bush declares war on 'Evil' Knievel

Robbie Knievel, son of Evel: 'Un-American'

WASHINGTON, Tuesday: US President George Bush has made his firmest commitment yet to stamping out evil in all its forms by declaring war against deceased stunt cyclist Evel Knievel.

Bush used the occasion of his State of the Union address to announce the campaign, drawing a standing ovation from Congress as he denounced Knievel's 'Axles of Evil'.

'America won't rest until it stamps out all acts of terror,' declared Bush. 'And watching someone jump through a ring of fire over three buses end-to-end is as terrifying as it gets.'

Bush said he was reluctant to engage in warfare against an American citizen, especially a dead one, but said the failure of economic sanctions against Knievel made the move necessary.

'We tried restricting his access to wrecked cars and buses. We even tried halting the supply of fifty metre ramps,' Bush told Congress. 'But Knievel persisted in his program of developing weapons of mass self-destruction.'

As further justification for his actions, Bush cited the presence of a suspicious white powder that had been discovered inside an urn with Knievel's name etched on it.

Knievel's son, Robbie, himself a renowned stunt cyclist, has defended his father's reputation by executing a spectacular 'wheelie' across the White House lawn. But the President condemned the protest as 'a cheap stunt'.

inside australia

the consulting industry

The Chaser ventures into the boardrooms and bars of big business and investigates the phenomenon of management consultants.

The term 'consultant industry' is itself a bit of a misnomer. Management consultancy is the antithesis of 'industry' which suggests the production or creation of a good or a service. Terms such as 'parasitic' or 'leeching' are perhaps more appropriate but have for some reason not been adopted by management consultancy firms.

Why do we have them?

Consulting firms first appeared as a response to a monumental crisis of confidence which overtook people in any position of authority, whether business or government, during the 1980s.

Consulting firms came in and convinced these people that they could no longer run their companies as they had been doing for years. Instead what they really needed was the advice of several recently graduated nerds who had never worked in any industry let alone the industry they were analysing.

The purpose of management consultancy firms is to defray responsibility. By engaging the services of a consulting firm responsibility is spread such that no one ever need own up. Managers need simply drop the name 'McKinsey' to justify any fuck-up they oversee while the consulting firms themselves simply blame 'poor implementation' or 'flat economic growth cycles that were clearly mentioned in the finer point of our advice'.

What do they do exactly?

Negative stereotypes of consultants suggest that they advise firms that to increase their profit they should sack half of their staff. This is not true. They also advise firms to sell infrastructure.

Consulting firms have grown on the back of the theory of 'outsourcing'. They are both paid to advise a firm to outsource and then employed to undertake the outsourced tasks.

What about their staff?

Management consulting firms are all about their staff. Their staff are their firms. Their firms are their staff etc. etc. ad nauseam.

To ensure they have the best staff, consulting firms only take the best of the best. Their recruits have often studied for years earning themselves PhDs, Masters and Honours degrees in fields from Engineering to Accountancy to Law. These recruits bring to consultancies immense knowledge which they are immediately told to forget. They are then taught how to make a graph in Microsoft Excel and how to change the colour and size of fonts in Microsoft PowerPoint presentations to send to their clients.

The Chaser

5 TIPS FOR BEING A GOOD MANAGEMENT CONSULTANT

1. UNDERSTAND the needs of your clients. Your clients need reassurance that they haven't wasted their money on hype wrapped in thinly veiled jargon, and hype. Accordingly, leaven your hype in thickly layered jargon.

2. ATTITUDE plays a part. Clients must feel like they are hiring people who they couldn't afford to hang out with if they weren't paying them $500 per hour. While to lawyers and bankers, arrogance is a personal vice that must be curbed in order to get work, for management consultants this principle is reversed. A humble management consultant is tits on a bull at four grand a day – don't waste your time or theirs if you can't walk the walk. They don't send you to Boston or Geneva to watch Training Videos 1 through 8 just so you can be humble, do they?

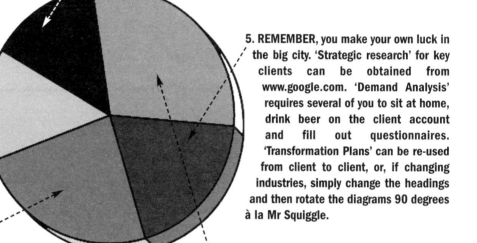

4. THEY aren't called 'clients' for nothing. When in doubt, remember that most businesses believe that they are inefficient and wasteful and deserve to be punished by suffering massive job cuts. They are like members of the House of Lords – however haughty they are when you first arrive, secretly they yearn for the lash.

5. REMEMBER, you make your own luck in the big city. 'Strategic research' for key clients can be obtained from www.google.com. 'Demand Analysis' requires several of you to sit at home, drink beer on the client account and fill out questionnaires. 'Transformation Plans' can be re-used from client to client, or, if changing industries, simply change the headings and then rotate the diagrams 90 degrees à la Mr Squiggle.

3. DIAGRAMS. These are your secret weapon. There is no concept too banal to be reduced to a flow-chart; no comparison so straightforward that it cannot be construed as an 'axis' (or better yet, a 'dimension'). A simple and obvious comparison between two things (like, say 'money going in' and 'money coming out') can be transformed with the right diagram from stating the obvious to 'throwing into relief a previously obscured causal relationship flowing from a new mechanism for interrogating this data'. The rule for business diagrams is simple: put it up there on PowerPoint, then 'Never Explain; Never Apologise'.

Management Consultancy Buzzwords

- ☑ **MANAGING INVENTORY: ensuring staff don't steal the stationery**
- ☑ **DISCRETIONARY SPENDING: how much of your personal booze can be charged to the client**
- ☑ **RESEARCH AND DEVELOPMENT: used to find out the highest amount the client can pay the consultant firm**
- ☑ **CREATING SHAREHOLDER VALUE: the Enron approach**

FIGHT CANCELLED

Tyson denied Nevada rape licence

LAS VEGAS, Thursday: Former World Champion boxer, Mike Tyson, will no longer fight Lennox Lewis in Las Vegas. The Nevada State Athletic Commission voted by a margin of 4-1 against giving Tyson a licence which would have permitted him to rape in the state.

The Commission issued a brief statement, declaring that in its opinion Tyson was 'not a fit and proper person to rape in the state of Nevada.'

Tyson – who was hoping to regain his title as Heavyweight Rape Champion of the World – was disappointed with the decision, according to his spokesman. 'We don't understand what the problem was. Mike had glowing character references from tons of people, like Rob Lowe, the San Francisco Ripper and Ted Kennedy,' he said.

'And anyway, Las Vegas is a state based on gambling, and with Mike in town, women could take the ultimate gamble.'

Commentators claimed that the decision was due to Tyson's initiation of a brawl during his press conference with Lennox Lewis during which he reputedly bit his opponent. 'Generally these Boxing Commissions will overlook something like a history of rape, but when you're biting another boxer or disrupting a press conference then things are really serious.'

Oliver Watts

22nd February 2002

Irish Bank trader loses $750 million: 'Waterproof teabag never caught on'

NEW YORK, Tuesday: John Rusnak, the Irish Bank trader who made losses totalling $US750 million, has defended his investments in a string of technology companies that all made substantial losses.

'I've just had the most unbelievable run of bad luck,' said a pensive Mr Rusnak. 'Who could have predicted that waterproof tea-bags wouldn't catch on? All the market research I did in Dublin suggested that the company was on to a real winner.'

Mr Rusnak attributed the failure of a defence contractor which manufactured flyscreens for submarines to the short-sightedness of US Navy officials. 'Sure, the product did have some problems in the testing phase, but if the US Navy had committed to the project as much as the Australian Navy did, flyscreens would be standard on all submarines today, not just the Collins-class.'

But Rusnak was mystified by the failure of a joint-venture that manufactured pedal-powered wheelchairs. 'We made thousands – and not one sold! Sheesh. You'd think that paraplegics would be more interested in fitness products.' The company was a joint venture between the Irish Bank and the Polish Bank.

Other products that Mr Rusnak invested in included an air-conditioning system for motorbikes, a solar powered flashlight and an inflatable dart board. His investment in a company which made ejector seats for helicopters is the subject of a Federal Aviation Authority inquiry. 'Actually, that was my idea,' he said. 'I came up with that idea while I was standing in a bar. Then this Scotsman and Englishman came in. We got up to some crazy antics that night.'

Mr Rusnak, who has been sacked from the Irish Bank, is philosophical about his investment failures and is now writing his first book, *How to Read*.

John Rusnak: claims the luck of the Irish has failed him

The Chaser

Ponting calls for new 'bonus pint' system

PRETORIA, Monday: The new Australia one-day international captain Ricky Ponting has shocked the cricket world with a bold new proposal – a bonus pints initiative.

'You want incentive to score quickly? I know I'd personally be swinging wilder than Warnie if I knew there were a few brewskis waiting for me in the shed,' Ponting announced. 'And if the ACB wanna keep captains honest, there's nothing more sure to encourage honesty than a shitload of alcohol.'

The suggestion has been applauded by cricket luminaries such as Dougie Walters and Rod 'Bacchus' Marsh. However, Walters added, 'I still reckon we should have gone with the bonus punts initiative I've been suggesting for all these years and quite frankly I'm surprised "Punter" Ponting hasn't seen things my way.' Shane Warne and Mark Waugh have also expressed their support of the bonus punts model.

The proposal comes after days of intense speculation over Ponting's fitness for captaincy, given his chequered past. But Ponting defended himself at the Australian team's new sparring facility, Kings Cross' Bourbon & Beefsteak Bar, telling reporters, 'People said I had a problem with alcohol, but that was crap. I just had a problem with that fucking bouncer.'

'I really have matured in the last few years under Steve Waugh's tutelage. Steve taught me that sometimes when things don't go your way you need to be patient and sledge people for a while before you glass them.'

'I want to be a captain in the mould of Steve Waugh,' Ponting continued. 'So I'll make a special effort to lose to New Zealand and swear at journalists. I just wish I had a twin brother who was past his prime.'

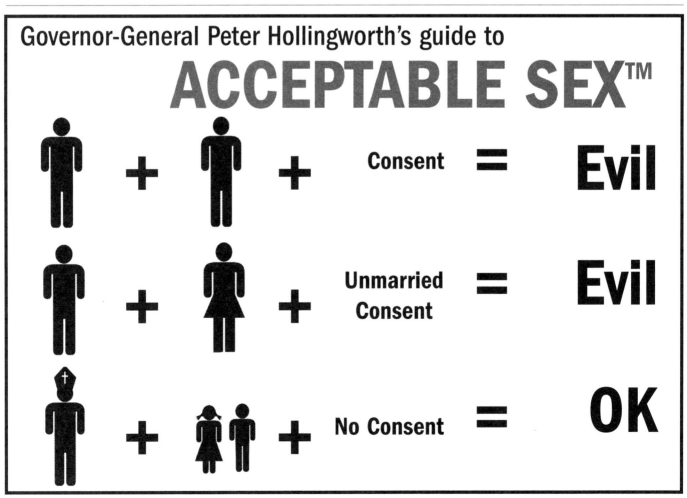

FBI warns of imminent terrorist warning

WASHINGTON, Friday: The FBI has issued the American public with a chilling warning that it could issue a terrorist warning some time soon.

FBI spokesman Chris Jenkins told a packed press conference today, 'It has come to our attention from unnamed sources that any of a number of acts may occur at an undisclosed location by unidentified persons employing a variety of means. As a result of this new information we are upgrading our idle speculation about a terrorist warning to a full warning of a warning.'

Concerns have been rife since fertiliser and petrol, possible ingredients of a rudimentary explosive, were discovered in an Arab–American's garden shed. A man has been taken into custody and a manhunt has begun to establish his lines of supply.

This is the eighth 'terrorist warning' warning the FBI has released since the September 11 attacks but Jenkins cautioned against complacency. 'The most horrendous aspect of the cowardly attacks on September 11 was that they were without warning. We guarantee that will never happen again.'

Jenkins followed his warning of a terrorist warning with a word of advice to those driving on wet roads and a caution to parents with pools in their backyards.

The announcement coincidentally came two hours before the FBI applied for an extra $300 billion grant from Capitol Hill. Responding to questions from the press about the propriety of the earlier warning, spokesmen declared the press 'un-American' and brandished American flags to riotous acclaim.

Prince Harry caught smoking Margaret's ashes

Harry and Margaret at the funeral

BALMORAL, Friday: Royal insiders report that the funeral of Her Royal Highness Princess Margaret was marred when young Prince Harry was discovered at the wake rolling fat joints out of her ashes.

It is understood that Harry smuggled Margaret's urn and some Tally-Hos to an outside stable where, joined by the Queen Mother, he settled in for a session. The high blood-alcohol content of Margaret's ashes not only ensured easy lighting, but had the peculiar effect of making those who smoked them drunk, rather than high.

The royal funeral was an otherwise stately affair, with tributes for the Princess pouring in from all those who loved her, and also from the Queen. Royal watchers described Margaret's death as a terrible loss, especially to the liquor industry.

In an official statement from the Palace, the Royal Family said the only positive side to the entire tragedy was that Elton John did not sing at the funeral.

Police demand more macho name for 'Taskforce Jenny'

Chalmers: creative control at stake

SYDNEY, Tuesday: Superintendent Nick Chalmers of the Wentworthville District Patrol has been stood down amid allegations that he named police taskforces without flair, imagination or metaphorical significance.

Chalmers is under particular fire for his naming of an arson taskforce. Commissioner of Police Peter Ryan deemed the name Taskforce Jenny 'entirely inappropriate, and, quite frankly, drab'. Instead, Ryan would have preferred to see the name Taskforce Phoenix, Operation Firebrand or Taskforce Cedar.

'I particularly like the name Taskforce Phoenix', Ryan said. 'It's evocative yet subtle and I think the classical allusion is a nice touch. It is true that our officers will not be collecting "cinnamon and spikenard, and myrrh" as Ovid described, nor will they be carrying a nest to the city of Heliopolis in Egypt and depositing it in the temple of the Sun, as the Phoenix was known to do, but at least it is a better name than Taskforce Jenny.'

The compromise name that Chalmers put forward – Taskforce Eastern Spotted Quoll – was flatly dismissed by Ryan in mediation yesterday and Chalmers' future remains unclear. Speaking at a press conference yesterday, Chalmers claimed that 'the issue is really one of creative control'.

Commissioner Ryan responded, 'I can accept that a Superintendent has the right to choose a taskforce name – to play around with words and really jazz things up – but it has to be done within reason. If a name without any metaphorical resonance is chosen, it should at least sound brave and manly. I would have found the names Taskforce Condor, Taskforce Cruiser or Operation Blue Steel entirely appropriate but girls' names are just so not us.'

Sully to host all Ten programs

SYDNEY, Thursday: Channel Ten plans to re-title every one of its programs for the rest of the 2002 season.

Henceforth, Channel Ten will attach to each of its programs the prefix, *Sandra Sully Presents.*

So far, media personality Sully has demonstrated her expertise on a vast range of intricate subjects by 'presenting' documentaries such as Sandra *Sully Presents the Human Body, Sandra Sully Presents the Planets,* and *Sandra Sully Presents the Battle of the Sexes.*

Now, all Ten programs will benefit from Sully's wealth of knowledge. *Sandra Sully Presents Yoga, Sandra Sully Presents Jerry Springer, Sandra Sully Presents The Bold and The Beautiful, Sandra Sully Presents the Simpsons,* and *Sandra Sully Presents This Is Your Day With Benny Hinn* are just a handful of the new programs on offer.

We can also look forward to a repeat broadcast of *Sandra Sully Presents the Human Body.* This time it will be entitled *Sandra Sully Presents Sandra Sully Presents the Human Body.* In each episode, Sully will introduce herself, who will then introduce the documentary.

Viewers are assured Sully will continue to employ her popular absurd, grotesque manner of enunciating ordinary words.

Schubert's Unfinished Symphony

Airline food success persuades Neil Perry to serve Rockpool meals in cardboard boxes

SYDNEY, Tuesday: The positive response to Neil Perry's revamp of the inflight food service on Qantas has convinced him that he should now also use cardboard boxes at his flagship restaurant Rockpool.

In recent years Perry has revolutionised airline catering by taking the old, bland meals that used to be served in foil trays, and putting them instead into cardboard boxes.

The master chef and food consultant is now planning to introduce the box initiative at Rockpool, his three-hat Sydney restaurant that remains the jewel in the crown of the Perry empire.

'I'm very excited about this new opportunity to broaden the minds of diners, and to explore new cardboard possibilities,' enthused Perry. 'I don't think signature Rockpool dishes such as the blue swimmer crab omelette will lose anything at all by being brought to the table in a Snack-Pack box.'

Perry said other standout dishes, such as his mud crab ravioli with oxtail and rosemary jus, will be heavily influenced by what he's learned at Qantas. 'I'll divide the meal into different compartments within the box,' he said. 'So the crab will be in the stirrer pack; the ravioli will come in a vacuum sealed wrap that's impossible to open; and the jus will come in its own little UHT tub.'

Perry: keen to give Rockpool patrons that authentic Qantas airborne dining experience

AL-QAEDA INTERCEPTIONS: THE FULL STORY

The CIA has released a full list of intercepted Arabic messages translated before and after September 11 following admissions that they intercepted messages from Al-Qaeda members saying 'tomorrow is zero day' but did not translate them until two days after the attack.

Intercepted messages translated prior to September 11

▸ 'I'll pick the kids up from school'
▸ 'I'm on the bus, I'll be there in a minute'
▸ 'No, sorry, this is the wrong number'
▸ 'This cave is giving me the shits'
▸ 'No, sorry, I don't have time to answer a few short questions'
▸ 'Hold the anchovies on that Supreme, would you?'

Messages intercepted before September 11 but only translated afterwards

▸ 'Tomorrow is zero day'
▸ 'You take the North tower, I'll take the South'
▸ 'Is the Pentagon that five-sided building?'
▸ 'I'm on American Airlines Flight 11 out of Boston'
▸ 'Allah will wreak vengeance on the US infidels tomorrow at around 8:46 a.m.'

Michael Nyman releases latest variation of his one piece

MANCHESTER, Wednesday: Composer Michael Nyman has announced the date for the first performance of the latest version of his sole musical work. The announcement has set the music world abuzz with speculation about what instruments Nyman will use to play his tune.

Nyman burst onto the music scene in the early 1980s when he developed a popular repetitive melody which was strongly reminiscent of a less accessible Philip Glass work. Since then Nyman has produced a string of successful variations to the work which have been marketed as new pieces of music. His work has also

been used as the soundtrack for a number of movies, including three versions of Peter Greenaway's only film. The work reached an even larger audience in 1993 when it was used in *The Piano*.

Making the announcement, Nyman spoke of his excitement about the new work. 'Composing this piece has been an amazing artistic journey for me, though I've mostly travelled to very familiar places'. He said that audiences 'can expect not to be surprised' when his work debuts.

Critics say it is only a matter of time before Nyman resorts to having his work played on the sitar by Ravi Shankar.

Nyman plans his next variation: 'Perhaps if they played it on the musical saw?'

NEWS EXCLUSIVE

CHILDREN OVERBOARD: Reith's damning new evidence

Former Defence Minister Peter Reith not only denies he lied about the children overboard saga, but now also maintains that the initial reports were true. To substantiate his claims that asylum-seekers threw their children into the sea, Mr Reith has released an stunning new photograph to the media. The image, he claims, has only just now been brought to light;

and provides incontestable proof that he was right all along.

Incontrovertible proof that the boat people ruthlessly threw their kids overboard

inside
australia

The Australian film industry

The Chaser rifles through the trash of some famous (and not so famous) people to present a revealing portrait of the Australian film industry and the hangers on it attracts.

The Australian film industry has a long and proud history of slumps and imminent revivals. The main responsibility of people who work in the industry is, in fact, not to produce films, but to produce tedious comment pieces for *The Australian* about the future of the industry and whether it reflects core Australian values.

Luckily, this is not a problem because the only people who go to Australian films are guilt-ridden middle class people who read the *Australian*. In reality, when Australians do get around to producing the occasional film it is always painfully mediocre. Thus, when you read about 'distinctly Australian' films, you must remember that what makes an Australian film distinct is its astounding mediocrity.

Sell out

With the establishment of Fox Studios in Sydney, many people believe the Australian film industry has simply become a branch office of all the major Hollywood studios, supplying high skilled labour at low prices. This is untrue. It has actually only become a branch office of Rupert Murdoch's Hollywood studios.

There is great debate over whether the Australian film industry will survive this shift, or whether it will be swamped by American culture. The recent wave of distinctly Australian films such as *The Bank, Risk* and *Welcome to Woop Woop* suggest that the sooner we're swamped by America the better.

The 'For an Australian Movie' Test

The criteria by which all Australian movies should be judged is known as The 'For an Australian Movie' Test. Whenever you are rating an Australian movie, you must ask yourself whether it was good 'for an Australian movie.' This test helps avoid the problem of comparing them with films from countries which are better at making movies than us. There are, of course, exceptions to this test. For example, the hit movie *Lantana* was so good that it didn't even feel like an Australian movie.

Funding

To make an Australian movie there are various state and federal government agencies that you can apply to for development funding. Simply fill out the forms (making sure the film in some way addresses Australia's problems in becoming a multicultural society or is about gay angst) and then submit it, along with a draft of the script, and a committee will review your submission and then – if you know John Polson – you will receive funding. It's that easy.

The Chaser

A Who's Who of Australian Cinema

RUSSELL CROWE
Got his big break playing Shirty, the Slightly Aggressive Bear for the D-Gen. He has been type-cast ever since.

NIKKI WEBSTER
Frighteningly, Nikki is about to launch her film career. She will be starring in a film called *Vanilla Gorilla*. There is hope, however, because the US Screenwriters' Guild strike has delayed the production.

JACK THOMPSON
Jack Thompson is the current 'Bill Hunter in Waiting'. He just needs to get a little bit crustier, and he's there. He has been doing those tree ads in an attempt to get more of a weather-beaten look.

BAZ LUHRMANN
Director of lavish films that are a little bit lacking on the substance side. Thank God his wife is a great art director, or no one would bother looking at his movies.

Genres

According to a self-regulatory code laid down by the Australian Film Finance Corporation, no matter what genre an Australian film is, it must fulfil the criteria of being 'quirky' and 'off-beat'.

Many people believe that another requirement of the code is that Bill Hunter appears in every movie. This is untrue. In fact, there is a Bill Hunter Equivalency Points System (BHEPS) which awards points for a series of Australian actors. For a film to be made, it must either have Bill Hunter in it, or have at least 100 points.

For example, Bud Tingwell is worth 50 BHEPS points, Bruce Spence is worth 30 and Michael Caton is worth 2.

Tropfest

Being one of the biggest short film festivals in the world, Tropfest is billed as giving an opportunity to up and coming filmmakers to demonstrate their skills. And it is true that some actors who appear in Tropfest films have gone on to have very successful careers in beer ads and mobile phone campaigns.

But the only opportunity Tropfest really offers is for various minor celebrities to get incredibly drunk once every year.

Incredibly Drunk

In the film industry 'getting incredibly drunk' is the phrase used to denote 'being fucked off your brains on coke'.

Sequels

Like the US film industry, the Australian film industry is not very good at sequels. Also like Hollywood, that doesn't stop them from being made.

Tina Turner was brought in to revitalise the flagging Mad Max franchise. This strategy was copied by the ARL, but with more success.

Aussie Stars

Aspiring young Australian actors are not so coke-addled that they don't understand that the only way they are ever going to get anywhere in their career is to leave Australia.

Aussie actors are very successful in Hollywood at the moment. Our male actors are highly valued because all the American leading men are either gerbil-fixated Buddhists like Richard Gere, or shoot blanks like Tom Cruise. This means that big, manly Australian actors are sought after as leading men in testosterone-starved Hollywood.

Australian actresses are also in great demand. This is because they are brilliant actors who are highly trained, beautiful and intelligent. This does not, however, explain Nicole Kidman's success.

Oscars Form Guide

The Chaser's guide to the nominations for the Academy Awards

BEST PICTURE

- Sweeping historical epic about a Big American Subject
- Preachy, sentimental film invariably starring Tom Hanks
- Miramax film whose publicists sent Academy voters the best foie gras
- Celebrated foreign film only here to make the Academy look progressive

BEST ACTRESS

- Washed-up forgotten actress making a poignant comeback
- Lightweight goofy starlet in her first serious dramatic role
- Token old dame of English theatre
- Complete unknown who apparently gives a bravura performance in a film no one has ever heard of or seen

BEST ACTOR

- Well-known actor who 'bravely' plays a homosexual
- Studio star who lobbied hard to play a retard
- Actor who uses lots of showy tics and mannerisms to indicate 'tour de force'
- A black actor

BEST DIRECTOR

- Critically and commercially renowned director who never ever wins
- Big name actor who now thinks he's a director
- Guy who draws attention to his direction by using lots of jump cuts
- Old director who boycotts ceremony over trivial grievance

[Note: inexplicable omission of director whose film has been nominated in every other category.]

BEST SUPPORTING ACTOR

- Guy who can't understand why he's not in Best Actor category, given he's in every scene of his movie
- Geriatric veteran nominated more for his prior work than for this unmemorable movie
- Heart-throb leading man who plays against type as someone 'ugly'
- Ed Harris

BEST SUPPORTING ACTRESS

- Scene-stealing best friend in otherwise forgettable romantic comedy
- Ensemble player in a Woody Allen film
- Cute 12-year-old girl in mature adult drama
- Surprise nominee who surprises everyone further by winning

BEST FOREIGN FILM

- Worthy film from Iran about a crippled boy
- Slow Taiwanese drama about papaya
- Quirky and surreal love fable from Eastern Europe
- Widely hyped film that's been a huge crossover hit

BEST DOCUMENTARY

- Sombre seven-hour meditation on the Holocaust
- Something examining an injustice against black people
- Documentary narrated by a slightly well-known actor
- Agenda-setting exposé on something of no real importance

BEST ORIGINAL SONG

- Soppy signature love theme sung by Celine Dion
- Gentle and unremarkable song by Randy Newman
- Something bland with lyrics by Tim Rice
- Inane, juvenile song from popular children's movie

BEST SOUND DESIGN IN AN ANIMATED SHORT

- Some person you've never heard of
- Some person you've never heard of
- Some person you've never heard of
- Some person you've never heard of, who wins and thanks more people you've never heard of

LIFETIME ACHIEVEMENT AWARD

- Senile, wheelchair-bound cinematographer who hasn't made anything decent for fifty years, but who gets a standing ovation anyway

8th March 2002

G-G DOOMED
Fox-Lew in charge of rescue bid

CANBERRA, Monday: The hopes of embattled Governor-General Dr Peter Hollingworth took a battering last night, after he learnt that the rescue bid for his survival is being headed up by Lindsay Fox and Solomon Lew.

The Fox-Lew consortium says it has a proud history of attempting to save Australian institutions that are clearly doomed. The pair has assured Dr Hollingworth that they will give him every impression that his position is safe, before unexpectedly abandoning him at the eleventh hour.

'We've told Peter we're absolutely committed to making this deal work,' said the wealthy Melbourne businessmen in a joint statement. 'Not only will we save his job and rescue his reputation, but we'll also be the first to deny any responsibility when it all comes unstuck.'

Fox-Lew said the rescue bid is dependent on securing vital leases at Yarralumla. The deal will also rely on substantial co-operation from the Commonwealth government. 'We're relying on them not to sack him,' Hollingworth's administrators said.

Lindsay Fox said the government has so far indicated its support for keeping Hollingworth in the air, but questioned whether their rhetoric might not contradict their real intention of keeping their options open and secretly wishing for a different outcome.

Formally launching their rescue bid yesterday afternoon, Lindsay Fox and Solomon Lew characteristically put on T-shirts that were far too small for them, and jointly squeezed their heads out of a tiny church window for a photo opportunity.

Analysts claimed that the rescue bid may fail due to a market oversaturated by gaffe-ridden liars.

'The government alone can sustain the public demand for leaders who continually let them down,' said one analyst.

A rival rescue bid for Hollingworth by Richard Branson's Virgin company is now unlikely to proceed, amid concerns that Virgins and Anglican Bishops rarely go together.

Fox and Lew at their launch to raise capital and expectations

Ariel Sharon apologises after 16 Palestinians die of natural causes

Sharon: promises the Knesset that such natural tragedy will never occur again

TEL AVIV, Wednesday: Israeli Prime Minister Ariel Sharon has been forced to apologise for the death of 16 Palestinians. The apology came after it was revealed to the Israeli Knesset that they had died of natural causes rather than as part of an overblown retaliation.

'I am very sorry that this has occurred and can only say that after our next strike on Palestine it is very unlikely to happen again,' Sharon told the Knesset.

Privately Sharon blamed moderate Foreign Minister Shimon Peres after he called for a halt in attacks long enough for Palestinians to do something to retaliate to.

'If we do not retaliate before we are attacked then many more Palestinians will again needlessly die of natural causes,' said Sharon.

In an effort to regain public support Sharon blamed Palestinian leader Yasser Arafat for the death of several Israeli settlers who also died of natural causes.

'We will bombard Arafat's compound at Ramallah every day until he arrests the Palestinians who are responsible for the natural death of these Israeli citizens,' said Sharon. 'If he does not arrest them it is further evidence that he supports the extremists on his side.'

This adds to an increasing list of demands which Arafat has so far ignored including that he arrest the Palestinian terrorists who stole Sharon's best cuff-links and made him forget his wife's birthday.

Claims by some European leaders that Sharon's demands are becoming unreasonable have been rejected by the United States.

'As long as he uses the rhetoric of a war on terrorism we will support any demand he makes,' said US Vice President Dick Cheney.

Girl disappointed real strawberries 'don't taste like strawberry'

GEELONG, Tuesday: A 15-year-old girl has told of her ordeal after eating real strawberries for the first time.

'I was a bit suspicious when I saw they weren't pink,' the girl told reporters, 'But nothing prepared me for what they actually taste like. They were nothing like strawberry ice cream at all – just weird and sugary, but in a lame way.'

The girl's grandmother only convinced the girl to finish the strawberries after lacing them with strawberry topping. However matters deteriorated further when the girl's grandmother offered her a lime.

'She kept on giving me so-called fruit that was horrible,' the girl continued, 'I guess fruit just tastes unnatural when it's not frosty.'

The girl, currently convalescing in the Canteen Wing of Geelong Hospital, has described the experience as her most disappointing since she tried to have a Bundy with a polar bear at the zoo.

Admiral Barrie finally informed of WW2 victory

CANBERRA, Thursday: The head of the Australian Defence Forces, Admiral Chris Barrie, said last night that he has just been advised about the Allies' victory in the Second World War.

Admiral Barrie said it was not unusual for the head of the military to be the last person to be informed of vital operational matters. He said he was also the last man to find out that Australia had a military at all.

The Defence Force chief said he learnt of the 1945 victory after ringing up someone who was involved in the campaign to ask how it was getting on.

'Up to that point, no one had ever told me what happened,' said Admiral Barrie. 'So in the absence of any evidence before me, I always believed what I wanted to.'

Admiral Barrie defended criticisms that he should have sought out information sooner, saying he was far too occupied attending to other matters which had come to light, such as the outbreak of the Great War.

Another opportunity for Fox and Lew to show their legendary Midas touch

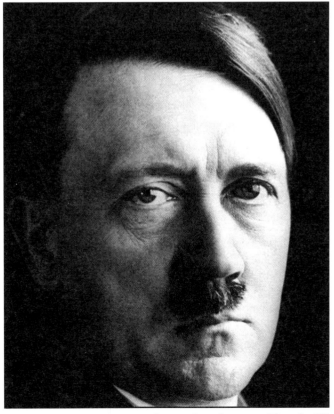

Hitler: evidence now suggests he may have lost war although still unclear whether he threw children overboard

Fox-Lew launch rescue bid for Beta video

MELBOURNE, Monday: Businessmen Solomon Lew and Lindsay Fox have shocked the finance sector with a daring bid to rescue the communications giant Beta Video.

Following their failed bid to save Ansett, the entrepreneurs have turned their attention to what Fox refers to as 'another once-in-a-lifetime opportunity.'

'I'm very excited about Beta Video's future,' announced Fox. 'If we stick together on this one, I reckon we can get this company back to the days it enjoyed a 0.3% market share.'

However, it isn't all smooth sailing for Fox and Lew's new Oedivateb consortium, with the government baulking at Fox and Lew's exhaustive list of demands, estimated as amounting to nearly $2000.

'Look, we're doing what we can to see this deal through,' said Richard Alston, the Minister for Communications. 'Obviously, we're desperate to save the six jobs associated with the company, even if they're only voluntary positions. But of most concern if Beta goes under is the potential for VHS to enjoy a virtual monopoly.'

The consortium's list of demands includes a government indemnity of the Beta work fleet's accrued entitlements, with Davo owed as much as $45 worth of Black Stump Restaurant coupons from last year's Melbourne Cup sweep and Trev owed a date with Kevin's sister after lending Kevin his Playstation.

The company's major creditors, Kevin's parents, who have loaned Beta Video the use of their basement for the last twenty-five years, are currently holding talks about the proposed acquisition but are said to still hold hopes for a partnership with the more reliable team of Jodee Rich and Brad Keeling.

The Chaser

Steven Bradbury awarded Ansett after other bids fall over

Prospective Ansett passengers are pleased with Bradbury's record for not crashing even when everyone else does

MELBOURNE, Monday: Charmed Olympic speed-skater Steven Bradbury has found himself owning Ansett, after all the other bidders unexpectedly wiped out.

Bradbury was never in contention to take over the beleaguered airline, but flukily ended up acquiring the asset when every other bid fell over just before the finish line.

'My plan was always just to hang back,' a jubilant Bradbury said last night. 'I thought if a couple of the bidders were brought down, then I'd have a reasonable chance of picking up a minor terminal or something. As it happens, I got the lot.'

Last week's failure of the Tesna consortium bid has affected thousands of Australians, not least Qantas shareholders, who are still celebrating the news.

John Anderson was disqualified from the race after he took out the other competitors as they approached the finish line.

Despite the disqualification the other competitors were still involved in a slanging match over who got in whose way.

'I was sailing into win comfortably until Fox and Lew cut the legs out from underneath me,' said Ansett administrator Mark Korda.

Former Ansett owner Gary Toomey was unusually candid when asked if the airline's problems could be traced to its awful TV advertising campaign. 'Absolutely,' he said.

With the Tesna bid shattered, it was assumed Ansett's only remaining hope was for Patrick Stevedores' Chris Corrigan to take over the airline. But Mr Corrigan said he was only prepared to run Ansett if he could use non-union staff and only operate flights to and from Dubai.

Virgin boss Richard Branson had also expressed an interest in some of the airline's assets, specifically its ten best-looking stewardesses, all of whom he's invited to his island.

The Chaser

Crowe allowed to sing at awards night: Viewers assault producer

LONDON, Monday: Thousands of British television viewers assaulted a BBC producer last night, after he screened an entire musical performance by Russell Crowe during an awards ceremony.

The viewers collectively dragged the TV producer into a basement and proceeded to verbally abuse him over his decision to air a whole song by Crowe's band 30 Odd Foot of Grunts.

The ambush follows a similar attack by Crowe on a producer who cut short his acceptance speech poem at the recent BAFTA awards. The actor also brawled with the telecast's clip producer who, during the Best Actor nominations, neglected to screen the entire movie for which Crowe was nominated.

'They only rolled about 15 seconds of it,' Crowe complained. 'Don't they appreciate the effort I put into these things? The least they could do is show one little film – it's not like I'm asking for a retrospective of my entire oeuvre or anything.'

The actor later made a point of being the kind of person who could use words like 'oeuvre', and at the same time still enjoy a VB as well.

In the wake of the BAFTA incident, it's understood the Oscars television producer is taking every precaution to avoid a repeat of the scuffle at

Crowe: singing to make his poetry seem more bearable

the British awards ceremony.

'I've decided to extend the telecast by another ten hours,' he said. 'You can't be too safe. Especially since I noticed the other day that Crowe was getting interested in Milton. And, what with Halle Berry digging *Beowulf*, it could be a long night.'

The Chaser

Berlusconi faces the tough set of questions he wrote for the media that morning

Surprise as Italian PM's media empire backs government

ROME, Thursday: Prime Minister and media magnate Silvio Berlusconi has told reporters he is pleased at the support his government has received in Italy's media. Mr Berlusconi, said he was 'especially pleased' that his own three commercial TV stations came out in favour of his new media policies, claiming 'it really could have gone either way'.

While Italy's eleven parliamentary Oppositions expressed concern about Berlusconi's proposal to remove all restrictions on the concentration of media ownership, the bill was also reported favourably in official Italian state media. The Italian public broadcaster had been critical of Mr Berlusconi in the past, but has been much more supportive since he returned to power.

Commentators outside Italy have suggested that the change is linked to the Prime Minister's power to appoint state television's board of governors. But Mr Berlusconi has rejected these allegations during a one-sided puff piece on *Italian Story*.

Mr Berlusconi defended his selections for the board and its controversial new chairman, Australian Jonathon Shier. 'He had an excellent resumé,' said Berlusconi. 'The suggestion that I chose him because he's a right wing toady is very unseemly, and certainly not the sort of question I'd expect from a career-minded journalist.'

Hollingworth dumped as patron of sexual abuser group

BURWOOD, Friday: The Governor-General has been forced to resign as patron of another organisation after Sexual Abusers Australia expressed concern about his attitude to child abuse.

'Following the remarks made by Dr Hollingworth on *Australian Story*, we feel his attitudes are no longer compatible with ours,' announced Vice President Grant Geller. 'We believe in molesting children, not vilifying them.'

'I recognise the years of faithful service Dr Hollingworth has extended to members of our group, especially his extraordinary efforts when Archbishop, but his position is no longer tenable.'

Hollingworth's comments, in which he implied that a 14-year-old abuse victim had displayed predatory tactics to seduce a priest, have infuriated several abuser groups including the Australian Catholic Abusers and the Violation Army.

'He's taking all the credit away from the child abuser,' said a spokesperson for the Violation Army.

Geller in his customary uniform

The latest indignity comes only days after Hollingworth was forced to cancel a visit to the Sexual Assault Ward of Long Bay Jail.

Hollingworth has remained diplomatic about the setbacks, wishing the groups well and re-iterating his commitment to covering up child abuse for the rest of his term.

Mardi
PHOTO

Just going through "confused stage"

THE ANGLICAN DIOCESE OF BRISBANE

GRAS
GALLERY

USING MARDI GRAS TO PUSH UNRELATED AGENDA

MEN WHO HAVEN'T TOLD THEIR WIVES

The Chaser

chase up ◆ HARASSMENT OF THE RICH AND FAMOUS ◆

NZ's own Russell Crowe got into a bit of biffo over a decision by the producer of the BAFTAs to cut his acceptance speech (and poetry recital) for the television broadcast. *The Chaser* offered him his own poetry column.

Russell Crowe
c/o Bedford & Pearce Management Pty Ltd
2/263 – 269 Alfred St
North Sydney NSW 2060

Dear Russ,

RE: OFFER TO PUBLISH POETRY ON YOUR BEHALF

We understand that you were a little annoyed the other night after the television screening of the BAFTA awards omitted the poem you had recited in your acceptance speech.

I really understand how frustrating it can be when people don't appreciate your artistic side (the other editors of this newspaper never ever let me publish my own sonnets in the paper).

And, so, although we don't generally publish poetry in The Chaser (it's a little too angst-ridden-teenagery for our tastes) we thought we'd make an exception in your case and offer to publish any poetry that you feel is not getting the publicity it deserves.

In return, the only thing we request is that 30 Odd Foot of Grunts never performs ever again.

Regards,

Charles Firth
Co-Editor
The Chaser

www.chaser.com.au
Phone: (02) 9380 5051 Fax: (02) 9356 8591

The Human Dimension

A CHASER SERIES

Far too often, the news doesn't give you all the news. Our feature column, the HUMAN DIMENSION, brings you a profile of someone who is influencing events through deeds, not words. The unsung heroes, the overlooked workers behind the scenes, the guy who hands the spanner to the guy who gets the medal for being the guy with the spanner in his hand.

Today we delve into the professional life of Angela Byrd, the office manager for neo-Nazi group 'Brothers in White Supremacist Rage'.

Membership has its privileges

Angela Byrd didn't set out to get mixed up with Montana Nazis, but the jobs at Starbucks were all taken. 'That's my story, and I'm sticking to it!' she exclaims, when anyone expresses doubts that simple economics and the pressures of unemployment could have led her to her current situation.

Byrd, 31, a former librarian and university-trained database manager, works as the membership secretary for Project 7. She is prepared to concede that as far as jobs for membership secretaries go, P7 is a little off the beaten track. 'I was really poor, and I thought of doing all sorts of different jobs to make ends meet. At one point, I was ghost-writing term papers for college students – they send you a credit card number and an assignment, and you email them back a term paper. But the assignments kept getting harder and harder and I spent all my time reading textbooks and trying to understand the questions being posed. One day it suddenly hit me that this was just ridiculous. If they aren't prepared to put in any work learning about the subjects they're studying, why should I? When the P7 thing came up, they said they needed someone who could get their computer to work, make the office a bit neater, and wouldn't rat them out to the UN One World Government conspiracy.'

Angela's immediate boss Brad Hitler

Byrd is clinical and professional about her role – to make sure that the membership database is accurate, that information about each of the 'Brothers in White Supremacist Rage' is up-to-date, and that mail-outs and other contact with the members go well. She characterises her role as being something of a facilitator. 'Sure, their approach to politics isn't my cup of tea, but a job is a job. Besides, it's a bit of an each-way bet – if they do prove to be the lunatic misanthropes and hillbillies that they seem to be, well, heck, their money is as good as anyone's – and if they overthrow the UN and reduce Washington to a pile of smoking rubble and establish the glorious true anarchic social state that they believe that the Founding Fathers intended before the Jews swapped drafts of the Constitution on them, well, I'm kind of in at the ground floor, which is nice.'

Project 7, a self-described 'community work project' based in Kalispell, Montana, leapt to international prominence earlier this week, when the *New York Times*

Just an ordinary day at the office for Angela (at front wearing sunglasses)

described the group as a 'far-right militia cell' and 'far fuller of creeps, weirdos and Bible-bashing gun-nuts than even small town community groups in Montana have a right to expect.' The group received blanket coverage for

its plan to bring down the US Government by assassinating all of the local law enforce-ment and Government officials in their small country town. As the local police chief described the plot to the *NYT*, 'the logic of their plan ... was that by killing local enforcement people, the state of Montana would have no choice but to send in the National Guard ... Then they hoped to wipe out the National Guard; and then they hoped that NATO troops would be sent in and that would trigger all-out revolution.' Although the primary planning stages of this plan have now been revealed in a major national newspaper, Project 7 has not yet formally renounced the plan. Byrd herself thinks it is unlikely now. 'We don't exactly have the element of surprise now,' she remarks dryly.

Membership secretarial work for the group originally consisted of maintaining a single Word document mailing list – basic work 'like regular

word-processing but with that really tricky mail merge stuff that you never get quite right,' as Byrd tells it. 'The biggest difficulty, frankly, is that the people I work with are generally uncomfortable with the organisational structures

> *'They needed someone who could get their computer to work, make the office a bit neater, and wouldn't rat them out to the UN One World Government conspiracy'*

necessary to get this stuff done. These are people, after all, who react with a plan to commit homicide when facing the need to obtain licences for their pets. I told them that I wanted everyone to fill out a membership form and I got all this crap about tattoos and

barcodes. What was that about? And as for telling them that we needed to keep tabs on members – well, let's just say that one of the perks of working for Project 7 is free ammo, and people use it. But generally, it was just a regular job, getting the mailouts done and chatting with people over the water-cooler about silly stuff, like the new series of *Friends* or how three international banks control the entire plastics industry or the best way to falsify a concealed weapon permit using a Montana Board of Education child's bus pass and a Magic Marker.'

All that changed when the group took its place on the international media stage. 'That was a pretty difficult day for us,' concedes Byrd, who will not admit to any specific membership figures for the group. 'We generally get new memberships through on-line applications, personal introductions, things like that. In the four months I'd been in the job, I'd processed, like, a couple of dozen new

members. But when the *New York Times* story came out, things went crazy!' She and a small team of membership secretarial consultants kept the 'White Power/Kill Faggots And Niggers.com' website running late into the night, as the membership ran from an estimated 50 to 61,000 in just over 24 hours.

Angela Byrd doesn't give the impression of being a Neo-Nazi or a crazed killer, and she takes care to distance herself from some of Project 7's more extreme views. 'Some of those guys, they're really out there,' she laughs, 'but we just get on with the job at hand. I mean, just because someone is busy hatching a plot to bring down the US Government by triggering a "grass-roots full-on anti-Communist revolutionary awakening" by gunning down some local security guards and a guy at the DMV doesn't mean they can get away with having a sloppy membership database. Professional pride plays a part too, you know.'

A successful mailout: this neo-Nazi rally was the first time Angela mastered the MS Word mail merge function

The Chaser

University O-Week Quiz

The new university year has begun. To help orientate students about tertiary life and the current state of higher education, *The Chaser* prepared this fun quiz. Test your knowledge of campus protocol.

(The correct answers will be published at the end of the university year, after markers have completed yet another long and unsuccessful strike action in support of better pay.)

1. You would only visit the university library if you:
a) Urgently needed a book to plagiarise
b) Were cruising for casual sex in stack
c) Couldn't wait till Christmas to photocopy your arse
d) Now work there, having finally finished a 12-year Arts degree

2. The majority of people who go to college are:

a) Private school wankers who crave institutionalised life
b) Former Trinity students
c) People who find the 10 km commute from home an inconvenience
d) Feminist authors researching an overrated bestseller

3. The upside of the government's failure to fund universities is:
a) There's no longer money for turgid course handouts you have to read
b) Class sizes are now so big they stretch to the bar
c) Academics have less money to spend on bad clothes
d) It makes a good documentary for Bob Connolly

4. The person most likely to sexually harass you at university is:
a) Your philosophy tutor
b) The university's Sexual Harassment Officer
c) The visiting Governor-General
d) A college boy

5. Entry to university is no longer based on merit, but rather on:
a) Whether or not you're Ian Thorpe
b) How much money you have
c) How much additional money you're prepared to donate
d) Whether your father is Kevan Gosper

6. You know you mustn't be watching a university drama production when:
a) The play makes sense
b) The actors are clothed
c) The quality's not too bad
d) There are people in the audience

The Chaser

7. As a general rule, the subsidised food at university:
a) Isn't actually food
b) Has been sitting in the bain-maries since 1970
c) Wouldn't even be spat on if it was served at Camp X-Ray
d) Is popular with engineering students

8. The most frustrating person in every tutorial is:

a) The slow, redneck guy wearing boat shoes
b) The shy, quiet girl who never says anything
c) The Marxist lesbian who never shuts up
d) The mature age student

9. You meet a new first-year student at an O-Week party. You immediately identify them as a tosser when they tell you:
a) They're doing Arts/Law, but only because they got the marks
b) They deferred first year to spend a year in London
c) They're already planning to direct the faculty revue
d) They're a member of the Young Liberals

10. To obtain maximum credibility at university, it's important to:
a) Never go to lectures
b) Become briefly bisexual
c) Reject your membership offer to the Golden Key Society
d) Turn up to your graduation naked

11. The greatest irony of university life is:
a) Ethics lecturers always sleep with their students
b) Psychology students are always fucked in the head
c) Debaters all agree about their brilliance
d) The Faculty of Architecture building is dog ugly

12. University O-Weeks are only worth attending to:
a) Get the free condoms in the enrolment showbag
b) Check out the new first-year talent
c) Hand in the essay that was due the year before
d) Confirm there's no need to attend again until the exams

Newsagency not a friggin' library

WILLOUGHBY, Tuesday: In a shock for Willoughby locals newsagent Clem Wilkinson today claimed that the High Street Newsagency was not, as previously believed, a library.

The controversial claim was made by Clem when he shouted 'this isn't a friggin' library' to three local youths hanging around the adult section.

In a statement issued by his lawyer Wilkinson said that he had been forced to put his foot down noting that 'no one is going to buy *Picture* magazine when they've already seen the centrefold.'

Wilkinson has since been unavailable for comment, his lawyers refusing to deny rumours that he is on the paper run.

Fiona Katauskas

Rebuilding

New York City Hall has announced plans to rebuild the Manhattan skyline in the wake of the September 11 terrorist attacks. Residents of New York have been asked to choose between four designs competing for the redevelopment tender.

Design 1:
Architects: Bush & Bush Partners

The Chaser

New York

Design 3:
Architects: Big Tobacco (Marketing Division)

Design 2:
Architects: Al Qaeda & Associates

Design 4:
**Architects: Federation
Square syndicate (Melb)**

22nd March 2002

Heffernan evidence conclusive: Proves he's an idiot

SYDNEY, Monday: The evidence released by Senator Bill Heffernan to substantiate his allegations against Justice Kirby have proved conclusively that the senator is an idiot.

'I don't care how many times he sends it to us,' said NSW Police Commissioner Peter Ryan. 'It's still just one dodgy statutory declaration and a CommCar receipt proving that he once visited the suburb of Darlinghurst.'

Sen. Heffernan defended his evidence, and the process by which he collected it. 'Everyone knows that whenever a CommCar goes to Darlinghurst, it's invariably visiting the Wall,' he said. 'Mine always does. I go down there every couple of weeks to try and find some desperate kid who'll sign a statutory declaration without reading it,' he said.

Heffernan's lack of evidence against Kirby left the government with their backs to the wall, and they have ordered Heffernan back to the Wall to try and save their position.

Despite the dodginess of the evidence, the Prime Minister has stood closely behind Heffernan. The Senator is said to be very nervous about this, but denies being in any way homophobic.

TRAVEL RECORD	COMMCAR		
DESCRIPTION MISGUIDED CRUSADE		NAME OF TRAVELLER SEN	
...SON FOR TRIP HOMOPHOBIA		POSITION HELD PM's R	
...E COMMENCED 1996	DATE FINISHED SOON	RELATIONSHIP T...	
PLACE ACTIVITY UNDERTAKEN	NATURE OF ACTIVITY / ITINERARY		
...E WALL	STAT. DEC FROM KNOWN PERJURER + UNRELIABLE WITNESS		
...YDNEY	MET WITH KATE WENTWORTH FOR MORE VAGUE EVIDENCE		
...ANBERRA	PARL. HOUSE FOR QUICK ABUSE OF PARL PRIVILEGE.		B
...CT P.O.	SEND ALREADY REJECTED EVIDENCE TO NSW POLICE		1...

Damning evidence: Heffernan's own CommCar records

The Chaser

Bush agrees to slash nuclear stockpile by firing it at Iraq

WASHINGTON, Tuesday: After months of pressure from the international community US President George W. Bush has agreed to slash the nuclear stockpile.

'Next week I plan to cut our nuclear stockpile by several hundred by firing them at Iraq,' said Bush.

Bush added that he would be willing to make greater reductions to the stockpile depending on the actions of other nations.

'We won't stop our reductions here. Right now I'm waiting for North Korea to give me a reason to reduce it further,' said Bush. 'Any reason at all, no matter how small, will do.'

Bush's announcement received a cool response from the anti-nuclear community.

'We're not quite sure whether this is entirely within the intent of the Nuclear Disarmament Treaty,' said a UN spokesperson.

But Secretary of Defence Donald Rumsfeld claimed that the plan was an improvement on the current UN backed sanctions.

'Nuclear weapons will kill millions of innocent people and Saddam Hussein whereas the current sanctions only kill the millions of innocent people,' said Rumsfeld.

The announcement came in a week when the leaked US Nuclear Posturing Report suggested that the administration was considering using nuclear weapons against nations without nuclear capabilities of their own.

'By targeting nations without nuclear weapons we are actually making nuclear warfare much safer,' said President Bush. 'At least for people in the US.'

Secretary of State Colin Powell also defended the policy claiming that it was not much of a change from the Cold War policy based on deterrence through mutually assured destruction, commonly known as MAD.

'We've improved upon MAD. Now we only nuke countries when we are really mad,' explained Powell.

But in response to continuing international complaints Bush settled to only use nuclear weapons in the event of extreme situations, such as in the event of his popularity rating falling below 40%.

Bush says his plans to attack Iraq simply take the START treaty literally

The Chaser

Souths to return to courtroom, the site of their only recent victory

Souths demand Federal Court overturn their 40-6 thrashing

REDFERN, Monday: Lawyers for South Sydney Football Club have initiated proceedings in the Federal Court seeking to overturn a decision by the National Rugby League awarding their first game of the season to Easts 40-6. Souths claims that the score reflected unfair criteria established by the NRL and News Limited to disadvantage Souths.

'The score of this game reflects an unfair criteria which is intended to exclude Souths from winning in the NRL competition,' said Souths' counsel Tom Hughes. 'The criteria unfairly favours teams who are supported by News Limited and who are able to score tries.'

Lawyers for the NRL and News Limited claim the score simply reflected the fact that Easts scored eight tries and six goals while Souths managed only one converted try.

Souths Chairman George Piggins claimed that the result

was unfairly decided by three people hand picked by the NRL.

'These so called referees had a biased view of the game and I have signed affidavits from 20,000 people at the game who saw things differently,' said Piggins to the cheering crowd.

In a surprising turn of events prominent Souths supporter and radio broadcaster Alan Jones disagreed with Piggins. Reading from a statement prepared by his lawyers, Jones said the game had been 'admirably and subjectively refereed by Bill Harrigan.'

Rabbitohs supporters will this weekend march on Town Hall in a rally to overturn the scoreline.

'I've been a Souths supporter since 2000 and this is the first time I can remember a decision like this going against us,' said one fan resplendently dressed in red and green. 'Mind you I have never seen a court case as violent as that either.'

Mugabe voted Miss Zimbabwe: Denies election was rigged

HARARE, Monday: The newly re-elected Zimbabwean President, Robert Mugabe, has officially been crowned Miss Zimbabwe, describing his triumph as 'a victory for black fashionablism'. But the victory comes amid concerns that the judging process may have been tainted.

Several members of the nine-man judging panel expressed surprise at the 438 to 9 vote outcome. However, the 78-year-old Mugabe explained the freakish result with, 'What I may lack in youth I more than make up for with bootyliciousness.'

Mugabe was warmly greeted by his supporters after the victory, including Miss South Africa and Miss Nigeria, who described Miss Zimbabwe's masculinity and long-lasting marriage as 'minor administrative oversights'.

The dictator raised eyebrows early on in the pageant, answering the question, 'If you were crowned Miss Zimbabwe what would you try to achieve?' with, 'World domination and the mass slaughter of white farmers.' But he easily won the field over in the talent section when he demonstrated his ability to exterminate all who

Mugabe: treasonably good looking

oppose his agenda, using two of the judges and all of his competitors as examples.

Fearing Mugabe may compromise the integrity of the beauty pageant, world monitoring body *Entertainment Tonight* sent several observers. Their interim report cited several instances of judges' free will being impaired, including descriptions of lengthy, desperate queues being stalled at the emergency exits just before Mugabe took part in the swimsuit section.

The report went on to warn that a failure to discipline Mugabe could damage the credibility of the Miss Universe Pageant as the pre-eminent beauty competition in the universe.

Anglo elders ask tourists not to climb Harbour Bridge

Anglo Elder Jim Higgins: 'It's a question of respect for our way of life'

SYDNEY, Monday: Australia's non-indigenous elders have requested that tourists stop climbing up the Harbour Bridge, out of respect for the significance the structure has in their culture.

The Anglo-Saxon elders said the bridge holds spiritual importance for their people, and that it shouldn't be recklessly trampled on by visiting hordes.

'We obviously can't stop people from going up if they want to,' said one urban elder. 'But we simply advise that we prefer them not to, and that it deeply offends our culture when they do.'

The original local riggers, who have lived on the land surrounding the bridge since 1932, have encouraged tourists to walk around the base of the bridge, as an alternative to ascending it.

'It's still a wonderful way to experience the bridge,' one elder rigger said. 'Although you will get a bit wet.'

Last year the New South Wales government agreed to close the bridge to climbers for one month, to allow the native urban inhabitants to mourn the death of former elder rigger Paul Hogan's career.

The Pope has banned the latest edition of *Playpriest*

Images of baby Christ arouse US bishops

ROME, Sunday: The Pope has issued a formal decree banning all artistic images of the baby Jesus, after learning that members of the US Catholic church were getting off on them.

Renaissance paintings and sculptures depicting the holy child will be removed and destroyed, as part of the Vatican's attempt to reduce the incidence of cardinal arousal.

'No one likes to rip up a Raphael,' explained one senior US bishop. 'But that's exactly what we've had to do, because Father Brennan can't walk past one without spoofing his robes.'

Another senior Boston priest was recently observed engaging in intercourse with Bernardino Fungai's *Madonna and Child with Saints and Angels*. 'I totally caught him with this 15th century diptych attached to his nob,' said a shocked colleague. 'He'd driven a hole right through the canvas. Imagine the cost if he was ever let loose in the Uffizi!'

Masterpieces by Renaissance artists such as Botticelli, da Vinci and Veronese have all recently been burned by papal decree, a move which has outraged the art world, whose auction houses hadn't yet finished colluding on the works' inflated value.

It's understood the Pope has also approved of Israel's recent destruction of the Church of the Nativity in Bethlehem, which contained so many depictions of the infant Christ as to make it a virtual hotbed of pornography for the average visiting bishop.

Despite the Vatican's determination to stamp out sex abuse in the church, the Pope said he would still morally prefer a child to be left alone with a perverted priest, than be raised by a single mother after IVF.

Pennsylvanian field owners overlooked in Sept 11 commemoration

SOMERSET, Tuesday: The owners of the field where United Airlines flight 93 crashed on September 11 have claimed that they felt neglected during the six month anniversary commemoration.

'Judging from the news coverage you would have thought that all of the inconvenience and tragedy of September 11 was centred on the World Trade Center,' said Jesse Williams Jr who grows wheat on the farm where the plane crashed. 'But we lost thousands of innocent bushels that day.'

Williams' wife Mary-Anne said she was annoyed that they were not offered funding for a tribute similar to the lights shone into the sky at the World Trade Center.

'We sat around all day waiting for the government to set up something,' said Mary-Anne. 'We ended up bunging a couple of torches into the ground and shining them up into the heavens. But CNN ignored our spectacular memorial.'

Citizens of Somerset are also disappointed by the lack of status that the town has achieved.

'We played a pivotal role in the day that the world changed forever,' said one Somerset citizen. 'But this place is as boring as ever.'

Williams too is waiting for a change. 'There seem to be

Williams says he doesn't need a memorial with the plane still there to remind him

hundreds of people working around the clock to recover everything from the World Trade Center site,' Williams said. 'But do you think they could find a single person to come and remove this plane from my backyard?'

Man begins to regret wacky email address

ADELAIDE, Friday: A 28-year-old Adelaide man is beginning to regret the humorous name he selected for his Hotmail email account. He said the address sexy_stud99 @hotmail.com is causing him increasing embarrassment.

'I use my Hotmail address for work quite a bit,' he said. 'And, yeah, I do get some funny looks from subcontractors and clients every now and then. I think they find it a bit childish.'

The man said he selected the name for a bit of a laugh, and assumed he would only be using the account for correspondence with close friends. But after going freelance two years ago, he suddenly found himself utilising the account for work purposes as well.

'It's especially bad when dealing with women clients,' he revealed. 'To be honest, I think they regard it as unprofessional.'

The man said he's already stopped giving out the address to women who he meets in bars, for fear of creating a negative impression. 'Yeah, I have to give them my Yahoo address instead, he said. 'Which is anal_fisting@yahoo.com. It's a lot more versatile I think.'

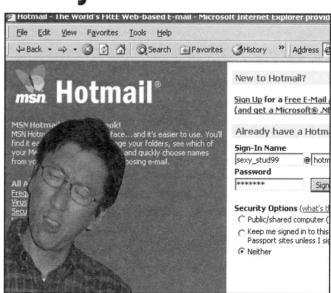

The 'sexy_stud': now a regretful_stud

Carey accepts offer to play with Brisbane diocese

Carey: training at his new club

BRISBANE, Monday: The disgraced AFL footballer Wayne Carey has accepted a lucrative offer to play next season for the Brisbane diocese. The diocese has signed Carey on a three-year contract, in the hope he'll add valuable experience to the church's sexual indiscretion line-up.

'He's a class signing,' said Archbishop David Aspinall. 'We're really happy to have him, and hope he can bolster our untrustworthy attack. I know a lot of people say his best adultery's behind him, and

he's not the philanderer he once was. But we're confident in this environment he'll be back to his best form.'

Aspinall said that since joining the Brisbane diocese Carey is feeling younger already. 'Or at least feeling younger girls,' he clarified. 'I expect we'll play him in the forward pocket of some unsuspecting schoolgirl. And with the Governor-General still providing great cover-up in defence, we're looking very strong for the up-coming season.'

Celebrity advice

With special guest
An email spammer

Q: Since I quit my job as a volleyball coach 3 months ago and started working as a sports administrator, I have gained more than 8 kg as I am much less active than I once was. Can you suggest some simple ways for me to shed this excess weight?

A: *****U can lose weight in your SLEEP!!!! Proven research shows BIO DYNAMIC PLUS can reduce fat by 23% and weight by 19%. ACT NOW!!! >> want to lose more fat?? Try our mail-order lipo-sculpture >>> minimal pain! Use in the comfort of your own home!**

Q: In the past, I have enjoyed a loving and passionate relationship with my husband of 16 years. Recently, I have found my sex drive waning and I'm not sure quite what I can do to turn things around.

A: **Adv: Increase sexual energy...we show you how. Prescription VIAGRA now available (free service). Now You Can Live The Life Others Only Dream Of. Or check out the **horniest sluts** on the net. Or Totally Shocking Barnyard Action – youngest goats permitted by law...**

Q: I'm bored with my secretarial job and I need to find a new direction with my career but I don't know where to start.

A: **Earn $88,673 p.a. working from home!!! We have spent the last 12 years researching home work options available to members of the public like You!!! You can live anywhere and work for most companies. The companies themselves can be located anywhere. U can earn **top $$$$** and slash your debts by 40%.**

The Chaser

Sept 11 widow discovers husband alive, remarried

New couple: September 11 a real break for their relationship

NEW YORK, Tuesday: A grieving New York woman, who's spent the past six months believing her husband died in the September 11 attacks, has now discovered him in bed with a 22-year-old waitress.

It's understood the husband, who worked in the World Trade Centre, knowingly let his wife assume he was killed so he could pursue his affair with a blonde bombshell at his local cafeteria.

'I wanted out of my marriage, and the second those planes hit I knew I had my chance,' he said. 'No divorce papers, no legal fees. Everyone thinks I'm in the rubble, while all the time I'm uptown in a motel room banging my brains out. Is that wrong?'

The husband's plan came unstuck after he eloped with his new lover to Wyoming, where the pair got married and spent time in the holiday cottage which the man shared with his former wife.

'How was I to know the missus would suddenly drop in?' he asked. 'It's Wyoming for christ's sake. She's supposed to be grieving for me. Who goes to Wyoming with a dead husband lying at ground zero? And – get this – she thinks I'M the one who behaved badly.'

German record store owner admits 'Vinyl Solution' may not be the ideal name

NEW YORK, Tuesday: Record store owner Dietmar Brumweiser, 26, originally of Munich, has admitted that his latest business venture, a record store called The Vinyl Solution, may be failing because of its name.

When Brumweiser opened Queens' first vinyl-only record store 3 weeks ago he thought the name was perfect.

'It suggests DJs can find any album they are looking for,' said Brumweiser. 'Get it? This is where to come for The Vinyl Solution.'

But he has been surprised that locals have been slow to warm to the name.

'Either they don't get it or they hate vinyl, said Brumweiser. 'I admit that the sound quality's not as good as on CDs, but I don't see

why these CD lovers have to go throwing eggs at my shop. Vinyl's a part of our history and there's no reason to be so hostile to it.'

But Brumweiser admits the unexpectedly hostile reaction of locals may force his business to close.

'It's very disappointing particularly given my previous failures in business,' said Brumweiser. 'I still wish my soccer sticker exchange shop, The Swap Sticker, hadn't gone under. Not to mention my night club The Lebens Room. And who would have thought that with the popularity of sports shoes in the mid-90s that my store The Third Nike, would have failed?'

The failure of the business comes at a bad time for the Brumweiser family as

Dietmar's wife's outdoor goods store, Mein Camping, is also struggling.

But Brumweiser says he will not be deterred by the problems he's encountered with The Vinyl Solution and

is already planning his next venture. 'I can admit that some people have a problem with vinyl, but everybody loves a yummy dessert. I reckon my Luft Waffles store will really take off.'

Brumweiser and his wife Helga in happier days, at the opening of The Vinyl Solution

ABC radio presenter covers story not in morning paper

SYDNEY, Monday: The presenter of ABC radio's 702 Sydney morning program, Sally Loane, took the unprecedented step yesterday of covering a story which she hadn't first seen in the *Sydney Morning Herald*.

The departure ends a three year institution on Loane's program, which tradition-ally bases its rundown entirely on news articles which the host has read that morning in her favourite broadsheet.

'She's fairly predictable that way,' admitted one of her producers. 'Like, before she gets in, you just know she's going to ask if we saw that piece on page 5 about Sydney's dining habits. We generally now know to line up all the same talent quoted in the article before she even asks us to.'

The producer said the *Herald*'s softer lifestyle articles particularly catch Loane's eye. 'Anything about the arts. Or real estate. Or debates about parenting,' the producer said. 'She's very comfortable with anything like that. Rugby's another pet topic. Anything

Loane: original story

but hard news basically. To cover that, she generally just does a phoner with whichever *Herald* journalist wrote that day's front page.'

The chef: frustrated

Thai restaurateur stumped for new 'Thai' pun

SYDNEY, Monday: Pip Pairoj, the owner of a new Thai restaurant says he can't think of an original pun to use for his restaurant's name. Pairoj was certain that every possible pun on the word 'Thai' had already been used.

'You look at it,' he said. 'Thai Foon, Thai Tanic, Bow Thai. All the great ones have been taken. What puns have they left me, so I too can have a cleverly named eatery?'

The frustrated owner said he has drawn up a shortlist of possible puns, which includes En-Thai-cing!, Mull of Kenthai, and Thai-Tarse.

'But I'm not really huge on any of them,' he said. 'I think at the end of the day I'll probably just go with Thai-some.'

SMH: read by Loane occasionally

Easter Showbag Guide

Anthony Mundine All Show Bag

- Anthony Mundine punching bag $12
- Copy of *Boxing for Dummies* $15
- Copy of *The Koran for Dummies* $15
- Total value $42
- **SHOW PRICE** $15

Wayne Carey Showbag

SORRY DISCONTINUED

- 2 packs of condoms
- 2 packets of gift chocolates
- 2 sets of double passes to the movies
- 2 bunches of roses
- 1 key to bathroom door
- 3000 reporters to place outside your home
- 1 person to make sure you don't commit suicide
- **SHOW PRICE** $15

Richard Carleton Showbag

- 1 x Copy of BBC documentary
- **SHOW PRICE** $15

Simon Crean Showbag

- 1 x soundbite*
- Comes with token female deputy!
- Guaranteed leadership challenge before next election
- NOTE: For rest of contents please refer to Liberal Party showbag
- **SHOW PRICE** $15

* Exactly the same one used ever since last election!

The Admiral Barrie Showbag*

- 1 Navy application form
- 1 Liberal party campaign strategy book
- **SHOW PRICE** $15

*Actual contents may not be as advertised

The Andersen Showbag

- A plastic bag full of shredded paper! $15

CLOSING DOWN SALE

The Chaser

Shafted Showbag

Hurry! Ends Soon!

- Actual replica of lever Red Symons uses to pull the plug on contestants
- Actual replica of lever Nine execs will use to pull plug on Red Symons
- Bonus video including footage of 'Fear Factor', 'Don't Forget Your Toothbrush' and the entire collected works of Tim Ferguson
- Total value   **$15**
- **SHOW PRICE**   **25ᶜ**
  (only while show lasts)

Miranda Devine Ratbag

- Blinkers   **$1**
- White armband   **$2**
- Vial of genuine vitriol   **$1**
- 1 idea*   **$5**
- Total value   **$9**
- **SHOW PRICE**   **$100,000**

* May fall apart when used

Bill Heffernan Showbag

- 5 blank stat decs   **worthless**
- Commonwealth Car logs   **worthless**
- A portable Senate Chamber (so that everything you say is privileged!)   **priceless**
- Only costs the career of a high court judge!
- **SHOW PRICE**   **$15**

The Al-Qaeda Showbag

- 1 novelty box cutter   **$5**
- 1 tea-towel   **$6**
- 1 novelty pilot's licence   **$2**
- 2 fun-sized explosive shoes   **$7**
- Total value   **$20**
- **SHOW PRICE**   **$15**

Darrell Lea Showbag

- 3 sticks of licorice   **$1**
- 5 sticks of musk   **$2**
- 3 sticks of novelty licorice   **$1**
- 5 sticks of novelty musk   **$2**
- 1 inexplicable baseball cap   **$25**
- Total value   **$31**
- **SHOW PRICE**   **$15**

Enron Showbag

- 100,000 shares
- Creative accountancy kit – let your imagination run wild
- Genuine Audit Certificate from Arthur Andersen
- **SHOW PRICE** WAS   **$80 billion**
- Now ONLY   **$220 billion**

The Jesus Showbag

- The only true Easter show bag!
- Actual fun-sized crucifix (includes nails)
- Crown of thorns
- Your Last Supper (Fun-size)
- **SHOW PRICE**
  Bargain! Only 15 pieces of silver.

* Resurrection on third day not guaranteed

The Chaser Showbag

- 1 newspaper packed full of gags and satire!
- 1 book packed full of same gags as newspaper
- 2 radio shows packed full of same gags as newspaper and book
- 1 website packed full of same gags as radio, newspaper and book
- 1 TV program packed full of same gags as newspaper, book and radio shows
- 120 bonus self-referential gags
- **SHOW PRICE**   **$15**

The Chaser

chase up ◆ HARASSMENT OF THE RICH AND FAMOUS ◆

While walking to our offices in Darlinghurst, *The Chaser* came across a huge number of these forms, floating out of the back of a Commonwealth Car as it drove past the Wall. Intrigued, we decided to reprint it here.

Dear Rent Boy,

Please complete the statutory declaration below, by circling the applicable responses, even where there is no truth to your claim. Please return the completed form to the office of the Right Honourable Senator Bill Heffernan, where it will fester in his dossier for several years, long after every police department has comprehensively discredited it. Additional copies of this form can be obtained from Kate Wentworth.

THE BILL HEFFERNAN
STATUTORY DECLARATION FORM
(PRO FORMA)

I, the undersigned, do hereby swear that I was anally raped by a High Court judge / Anglican archbishop / rotating combination of the two.

I am regularly engaged and paid to perform sexual services for _____

(office use only – Bill will find this bit out)

I strenuously deny that Bill Heffernan in any way coerced this statement from me / paid me handsomely to sign it / is a stark raving loon.

_____
sign here

_____
date

The Chaser

Carey says no to Swans: Vice-captain's wife not up to scratch

WAGGA WAGGA, Thursday: Wayne Carey has shocked the football world again by declaring himself off limits to the Swans, following a routine inspection of the wife of Swans' vice-captain Matthew Nicks.

A potential move to the Swans in 2003 has been mooted ever since Carey resigned from the Kangaroos in disgrace after his affair with the wife of vice-captain Anthony Stevens.

'I guess Mrs Nicks isn't that bad, but the fact that I'm not good friends with Matthew Nicks makes her much less desirable,' said Carey.

Carey was reportedly not only dissatisfied with the wives on offer in Sydney but also with the Swans' facilities. 'I found their bathroom security arrangements particularly flimsy,' Carey explained to reporters. 'Besides, I've always dreamed of playing soccer for Manchester United. Especially since David Beckham married Posh Spice.'

Swans insiders claim that the team may not have accepted Carey anyway. Swans vice-captain Matthew Nicks is rumoured to have conducted a vigorous campaign against Carey joining the Swans, a campaign which only intensified after Nicks found his wife showing

a distinct lack of support for it.

Carey himself would have no part in furthering such speculation. 'At the moment the most important thing for me is to make up things with my wife. I thought it would be easy, cause I've been making up things to her for years to hide my affairs. But I think

this is going to take a special effort – I may only have affairs with single girls for a while.'

Meanwhile Kangaroos Coach Denis Pagan is still picking up the pieces after the week's events. 'We've had to make a lot of changes,' Pagan told reporters. 'And the first one we made was to stop using Bill

Clinton as our motivational speaker. In hindsight, that wasn't a great idea.'

The Kangaroos are yet to decide who their new captain will be but Anthony Stevens is keen for the position, believing the promotion may convince his wife to have sex with him.

Carey: meets with his prospective team mates and team's mates

The Chaser

Queen Mum – a life tragically cut short

LONDON, Sunday: The world has been numbed by grief and shock, after Her Royal Highness the Queen Mother unexpectedly died last night at the tender age of 101.

The Queen Mum's life was tragically cut short when she passed away suddenly in her home at Windsor Castle. English mourners have gathered in large numbers outside Buckingham Palace, silently holding candles as they try to come to terms with the premature death of the popular royal.

'It's tragic that she should go so early,' said eminent royal watcher Sir Crispin Poncey-Poncey. 'She still had her whole life ahead of her, and by all rights should have lived to the ripe old age of 900. It just seems so unfair that we should lose her so soon.'

Tributes have poured in from around the world for the beloved monarch cut down in her prime. The British liquor industry is understood to be particularly affected by the loss. Gin retailers are nervous about how their businesses will survive now that their most loyal customer is dead.

'To lose both the Queen Mum and Princess Margaret is just disastrous,' said one purveyor of gin. 'Add to that the death of Dudley Moore, and you'd have to say it's not a good time to be selling grog. We haven't seen a downturn this big since Oliver Reed dropped off the twig.'

The Queen Mother narrowly averted an earlier death on a recent trip to Paris, where she was nearly involved in a fatal speeding accident on her Zimmer frame inside a tunnel.

In a final gesture to symbolise her love of horses, the Queen Mum has requested that her body be taken to a racecourse, dragged behind a screen and shot.

The Chaser

A World Mourns

'Her coffin looks like it was made by an Indian.'
PRINCE PHILLIP

'I am available for the funeral.'
SIR ELTON JOHN

'She touched us all. If only I could have touched her.'
PAUL KEATING

'This awful tragedy puts mine into perspective.'
AFGHAN EARTHQUAKE VICTIM

'She's the only person who made me look young.'
CAMILLA PARKER BOWLES

'She inspired me in so many areas of my life – primarily fashion.'
JANETTE HOWARD

'Don't look at me. I didn't do this one.'
PHILIP NITSCHKE

'She brought it on herself.'
DR PETER HOLLINGWORTH

'I don't talk to the media about discreet Royal matters...any more'
COUNTESS OF WESSEX, SOPHIE RHYS-JONES

'Well may we say God save the Queen, because nothing will save the Queen Mother.'
GOUGH WHITLAM

'I did not have sexual relations with that woman.'
BILL CLINTON

'What a great way to lose weight.'
SARAH FERGUSON

The Queen Mother: A lifetime of achievement

1900
Born

1939
Couldn't be arsed leaving London during war

2002
Died

The Chaser

We all know she's having a funeral. We all know why. But until now, we didn't know absolutely every minute detail about what would happen when. Now your obsessive fascination with the Royal Family can at last be quenched, thanks to *The Chaser*'s exclusive moles inside Buckingham Palace.

Order of Service
for the funeral of

HRH QUEEN ELIZABETH THE QUEEN MOTHER
1900 - 2002

Assembly
Remaining living royals congregate in chapel

Prayer of thanks
Led by the deceased's long-serving chambermaid, who no longer has to empty the royal bedpan

FIRST LESSON: Psalm 15
Old Testament reading by Prince Harry (giggling)

MUSICAL INTERLUDE
Elton John, 'Candle In the Wind' (Reworking III)

IN MEMORIAM
Ponderous rambling eulogy by pompous windbag toff

EUCHARIST
Congregation receives the gin of Christ

MUSICAL INTERLUDE
Elton John, 'Candle In the Wind' (Reworking IV)

SECOND LESSON: 1 Corinthians 13
New Testament scripture read by the Queen Mother's favourite horse

CLOSING PRAYER
Everyone resumes their holiday skiing in Switzerland

Palestinian Lifeline admits poor record on suicide

Al-Masri

And some more prospective callers

NABLUS, Tuesday: The president of the Palestinian Lifeline, Ghassan al-Masri, admitted today that the organisation's recent record was poor. The organisation was established one year ago to prevent suicide.

'I admit that, if anything, Palestinian suicide rates are on the increase,' said al-Masri. 'And we clearly have to take the responsibility for that.'

Al-Masri admitted that staff morale at Lifeline's Nablus office was at an all time low.

'The tough part is not knowing why this is happening. We've gone through the checklist and there doesn't seem to be an increase in relationship troubles or problems dealing with puberty.'

Most disturbing for al-Masri and his staff are the increasingly violent methods being used by suicide victims.

'We have made a slight dent in suicide using pills and wrist-cutting, but bomb usage is way up on last year.'

'We always say that people thinking of committing suicide should think about the harm they are doing to other people. But these people using bombs make it seem like they actually want to hurt other people.'

Man carefully arranges bedside novels before big date

MELBOURNE, Friday: A twenty-five-year-old Melbourne student spent more than three hours last night painstakingly choosing which novels to leave beside his bed, in order to impress his date.

'It was a first date, and I had no idea what she was into,' the young man said. 'I mean, do you play it safe and stick to the canon – Austen, Joyce, Flaubert? Or do you take a punt and put out some David Foster Wallace? Or some early lesser-known DeLillo?'

The student said he spent a good 40 minutes fretting over whether to include a book of verse. 'I wanted her to know I was across all the poets but – again – it was that fine line between looking well-read and scaring her off with something more modernist than she usually likes.'

In the end, he struck what he regarded as a sensible balance between the quality mainstream and bibliophile esoterica by displaying a well-thumbed paperback Camus, a recent Martin Amis and a first edition Dario Fo in translation.

He additionally left lying on the bedroom floor, in a calculatedly messy fashion,

Hours spent making book look thumbed

copies of the *Guardian Weekly* and the *New Yorker* magazine. On top of his CD player, he casually stacked recent records by Radiohead, Ryan Adams and Gomez. 'And some Charles Mingus just to prove I dig jazz too,' he said.

The student revealed that, after all that, his date didn't end up coming back to his place anyway.

Virtual unknown replaces virtual unknown as NSW Liberal leader

SYDNEY, Thursday: NSW has a new opposition leader after virtual unknown John Brogden won the leadership from virtual unknown Kerry Chikarovski.

Brogden launched the challenge as a desperate last-ditch attempt to save the Liberals from certain defeat at the next election under Chikarovski. The Liberals now face certain defeat at the next election under Brogden.

Chikarovski defended herself from claims that she had never polled above 19% as leader, saying 'They said that about Alexander Downer, too.'

Mr Brogden said that Chikarovski still had a lot to offer the party. When pressed to name what she has to offer, he said 'Well, she's very good at looking as though her face is pressed up against a glass pane.'

'Fundamentally, it was always going to be very hard for her – she got the job in a coup just before the last election, when we were always going to be defeated – especially with her as leader.'

At 33, Brogden has broken the record by being the youngest ever Liberal leader, and is tipped to go on making records by being the youngest ever former Liberal leader.

Brogden: unknown

Chikarovski: unknown

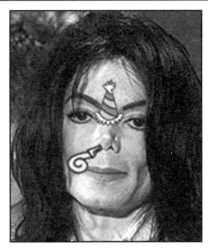

The lucky appendage on its special day

Michael Jackson's nose celebrates 21st birthday

LOS ANGELES, Monday: The stars were out last night to celebrate the coming of age of Tinseltown veteran, Michael Jackson's nose. Hollywood's A-list, from Angelina Jolie's lips to Britney Spears' breasts and Cher's cheeks, chin, eyebrows and butt came out to see and be seen at the glamour bash.

The nose welcomed guests with a short but elegant speech in which he thanked Jackson, 'for helping me get myself straightened out.'

'My nose had a troubled childhood,' a teary Michael Jackson explained during his speech. 'The paparazzi always hounded him, he often felt smothered by my surgical mask and he's had a few ugly scrapes with my plastic surgeon. Once he even ran away during one of my concerts. But we were soon reunited in a ceremony at Las Vegas General Hospital and now we've grown so close that he's almost a part of me.'

'We've both changed over the years but I think now that I've grown a bit and he's shrunk a bit, our future together's looking rosy.'

Jackson then proceeded to amuse the ensemble with some highly compromising anecdotes about what his nose and Diana Ross' nose got up to one night when they were off their faces.

Jackson with his former band and nose

The Chaser

Male Corr accepts he may not be the reason for the band's popularity

Jim Corr and his three female passengers

DUBLIN, Monday: The sole male member of the popular Irish group The Corrs yesterday conceded for the first time that he may not be the reason for the band's enormous appeal.

Jim Corr said he'd previously always attributed the group's success to his signature guitar sound and good looks. He said for years he felt weighed down by the burden of having to carry the group single-handedly.

'We were filling large stadiums, and I put it all down to me,' he said. 'I got the feeling the other three were really just riding on my name. So, yeah, there was a lot of pressure on me each night to please the fans – most of whom, for some reason, were young screaming men. I just assumed we had a big gay following.'

Jim said his first real doubts about the centrality of his role occurred on a recent tour, when the road manager stopped lighting his corner of the stage. Instead he was asked to stand at the rear of the stage behind the backing musicians. He noticed also that his face had been cropped out of the band's promotional tour poster.

'Small things, sure, but they all added up,' said Jim. 'And then when we turned up to a press conference in New York and the record company had only provided three chairs for the band, I started to get the hint.'

Jim's belated acceptance that he may not be the chief drawcard for The Corrs has forced him to momentarily put on hold his plans for a solo career.

Man admits April Fools murder 'took joke too far'

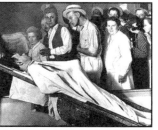

The prankster, still trying to explain the joke

WASHINGTON, Monday: A 42-year-old man who murdered an office colleague as part of an April Fools Day prank has admitted that he probably took the joke too far.

The renowned practical joker accepted last night that he went beyond the bounds of humour by killing his close friend and business partner in a jocular stunt which onlookers described as 'ill-judged.'

'I've always liked playing jokes on people,' said the notorious office wag. 'And I was determined to pull off a real doozie for April Fools Day – something that would have people talking for days. But I agree in hindsight that putting strychnine in Alan's coffee was a bit much – even by my standards!'

The prankster said he thought the joke was funny for a while, but became more serious when a coroner and police were called to the office.

Stem cell lab destroyed by explosion: Death toll arguably 60,000

PERTH, Wednesday: A devastating explosion at Australia's leading stem cell research laboratory has sparked intense philosophical debate over the size of the death toll. Scientists who worked in the building say that, although valuable stem cells were lost at the lab, it was unmanned at the time of the blast and no lives were lost. But religious activists opposed to stem cell research argue the explosion claimed 'approximately 60,000 totally valid little human lives'. The activists were also appalled by the lack of childcare facilities

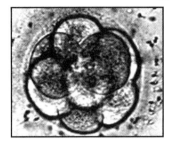

One of the deceased

at the research facility.

If the activists are correct, the explosion boasts the highest casualty rate since the bombing of Hiroshima.

The debate has divided the local community. Head of the local emergency services Cmdr Bill Flanagan has sided with the scientists. 'If we accept the Christians' version then the paperwork alone will keep me going for several years', Cmdr Flanagan admitted. Cmdr Flanagan's stance has been endorsed by leading sperm donor Roger Wellings who said he is 'horrified at the thought of losing my entire, apparently huge, family in one terrible disaster'.

But funeral directors and florists have sided with the activists, whose position they described as 'much more philosophically appealing, not to mention profitable'.

Local media have hedged their bets, reporting the incident as involving the loss of '60,000 almost lives'.

Officials at the hospital nearest the stem cell lab also faced a quandary in the aftermath of the explosion. 'Yeah, it was tough,' said hospital Registrar Phil Allara. 'The God Squad stormed into emergency with a couple of thousand cracked test tubes asking us to "save the children". But we had to tell them that we couldn't save them. At least not until we've done more research.'

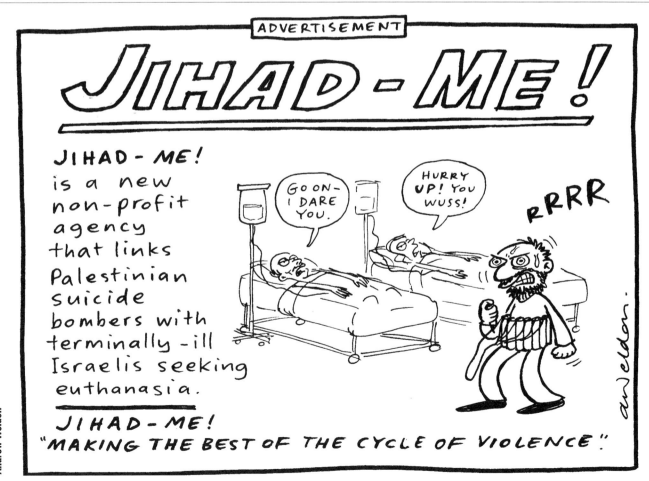

The Chaser

Cryogenic suspension
It's Fun! ™

WELCOME to the continuation of the article that appeared in the 30 March 1976 issue of *The Chaser,* 'Cryogenic suspension – it's fun!™.'

All that time ago, you selected a loved one or a dear friend for the privilege of being frozen in ice, only to be woken in the far future when the world will be a paradise free from disease and hatred.

In case you've forgotten, here are the most salient points of the 1976 Chaser How-To Guide™ for Cryogenic Suspension™:

Buy a large deep-freeze
When freezing a person, it must be done as quickly as possible, or else it won't be scientific. For this reason, turn the dial on your freezer to the highest setting, usually 9 or sometimes 8 or another number.

If you meet with complaints or resistance from the loved one you wish to suspend, perhaps claiming they know better than you, simply ease them into the freezer compartment by swiftly winding them with a length of chain, and then ushering them inside as they squeak and hiccup in an amusing attempt to draw breath.

Close the freezer door, and wait 26 years.

Remember those simple steps? If not, relax and read over them again.

Now it's time to resuscitate your friend or family member. 26 years have gone by, and they're ready to embrace the utopian future in which we now live!

Open the freezer, and remove the icy beloved. You can already help adjust them to life beyond 1976 by snapping off their frosty sideburns with your hands.

These make a delicious summer treat for the kids.

After thawing, your special person from beyond time will be disoriented and slightly delirious. Simply deliver to them the following lecture about the new, futuristic space-world of 2002:

Welcome to 2002, loved one
Many things have changed since your own dark time of 1976. Don't worry. I'll explain everything slowly.

Your colourful tattoos are now unacceptable. You must now sport only a spiky-looking black pattern tattoo, and then only if you're a girl.

Fortunately, for women, your flared jeans are now compulsory, although they were shunned for many long years. If you are a man, however, Christ knows what you're supposed to wear.

A career in computers is now more desirable than one in law or medicine. No, I am not joking. Yes, I said computers.

Yes, I said desirable.

It is no longer the fashion to copulate with girls under 15. Instead, we simply read and talk about it incessantly.

Czechoslovakia is not called that any more. Now, as a mighty and powerful new nation, it is called the Czech Republic.

The word 'impact' is now a verb.

Smoking can now give you cancer, but no one gives a bugger.

No one bought the latest albums by Mick Jagger, the Bee Gees, ELO, Bob Dylan, Paul McCartney, or Michael Jackson from the Jackson Five.

The mere presence of an effeminate gay man on stage or screen is no longer sufficient to make an audience laugh hysterically.

Having calmed your ice-person with the above advice, you will now have to

Top: A cryogenic tank
Below: A resident of that tank

make them accustomed to standing upright.

If the best they can do is lie on the floor in a puddle without breathing or moving, simply pop them back into the freezer for another 26 years.

We'll publish the next stage of this How-To Guide™ in the 30 March 2028 issue of *The Chaser.*

The Human Dimension

A CHASER SERIES

Today we profile Henry Myers, Executive Vice President of Interlink Industries, the largest manufacturer of razor wire in Australia

The 'genius' of capitalism

Every cloud, they say, has a silver lining. Henry Myers makes his living from one such silver lining – but where his products go, there are few clouds. As Executive Vice-President responsible for New Business Development for Interlink Industries, the largest manufacturer of razor wire in Australia, Myers has had a great year.

His products are soaking up the rays at Woomera and now at a new, 1200-person facility 200 kilometres north of Port Augusta in South Australia. Orders are flowing in – they have just signed a new, 3-year exclusive deal with the Department of Immigration and Multicultural Affairs to supply all the Department's need for barbed wire, wall-top spikes, 'directional matrices' for driveways (they're the things that blow the tires on a car going the wrong way) and, last but not least, over 600 tons of razor wire.

'We need to engage in what I call "demand management" '

And then there's the TV coverage. 'Obviously, we need to be sensitive to the context in which our products appear on TV,' Myers volunteers, 'but I have to say I felt, well, just swollen up with pride when I saw the distinctive coils of Prime GLM #4 [their flagship brand of razor wire] on the *National Nine News*. Although the camera was really panning to follow the man leaping onto the barrier, you could really see – if you knew what to look for – just how well our Sunproof® coating had kept the appearance of the product pristine. It just coiled back into shape when they pulled him off the wire – just like we promised the customer it would!'

Of course, Interlink Industries' Static Barriers Division doesn't just manufacture razor wire – they make over 100 varieties of barbed wire and other forms of ordinance necessary for the well-equipped detention centre. The problem with the industry is that demand for their products can be pretty flat. Myers is leading the charge to bring new values to the company. 'We take business development seriously at Interlink – I have a meeting with my team each

week where we really challenge each other to think 'out of the box'. After all, unlike people in sexy industries like computers or communications, demand for our products is generally slow-growing. So we need to engage in what I call 'demand management'. We need to identify those actions that the company can take to boost sales – it's a really creative role.'

Like many senior managers in corporate Australia, Myers cut his teeth overseas and is a graduate of a top business management school (he has an MBA from Wharton). Day to day, Myers and his team are responsible for ensuring that Interlink's orders keep flowing in – and the business environment is an unforgiving one. 'Basically, our product is imperishable, has no civilian or consumer use – although we're working on that – and is used for a single business application,' Myers explains. That single application, guest location management (or GLM), is the basic source of business that keeps Interlink and the 300 people at its plant near Newcastle above water. Myers' role is to make sure that demand stays strong and predictable – a subject vital to the management team at

The Chaser

Interlink. Until the recent upsurge in asylum seekers arriving in Australia, and the attendant need for further detention centres, Interlink had been staring down the barrel. In 1998, the stock had dropped 18% in six months, and talk of a take-over was rife. 'If it hadn't been for the people smugglers, we'd have been sunk,' recalls Myers.

Myers has pioneered a new, analytic approach to sales and marketing at Interlink. When he arrived he was horrified to discover that the business did little more than print a catalogue and wait for the phone to ring. 'That's no way to build a business – you are simply at the mercy of demand. You can't plan, and you certainly can't grow. So my job is to make sure that we can do both. And that means demand stimulation. It's like when Telstra runs those ads that are basically about how good it is to call people – so you pick up the phone. We analysed what led to a person in Canberra picking up the phone and calling us to order some razor wire. It turns out that a lot of things have to happen for that to occur – some of them political, some of them social, some of them to do with the procurement process, and so on. We plot it all up on a big whiteboard, and start looking for the bottlenecks.'

Some proposals are discarded as simply impractical – such as the idea of razor wire that would decay in the sun, like the UV-disintegrating shopping bags ('They'd just change brands,' remarks Myers).

The most successful 'vertical synergy' so far has been the purchase of ASA, a small savings and loan bank

A photo from Interlink's new ad that aims to put a human face on razor wire

based in Java. ASA targets start-up businesses in the fast-growing Indonesian economy and has delivered a healthy return despite both the currency risk associated with the rupiah and the bad-debt problems associated with the problem of failing businesses. Those that thrive, maintains Myers, have helped Interlink make a good return on their investment – and he dismisses stories about ASA money funding people-smuggling as 'absurd'.

Myers is careful to point out that Interlink deplores the practice of people-smuggling and opposes its practice (and, he notes, has not actively funded the teaching of its theory since 1999). On the other hand, he adamantly defends Interlink's right to raise maritime skills in South Indonesia ('essentially a charitable exercise'), offer micro-credit funding for unsecured personal loans to people with no credit history in major South East Asian countries ('in cash, and our

loan officers will visit you on the pier').

'It really comes down to personal responsibility. Say you borrow some money from the bank, and use it to do something wrong – like buy guns, or drugs. Is the bank responsible? Of course not. If we lend some money to a struggling entrepreneur in Southern Java, and that person uses the money to start up a people-smuggling operation, that's deplorable. I wish there was something we could do about that, I really do. But it's a whole other thing to be saying that the fact that this happens and that the number of people being put on these boats and then captured by the Navy and brought to these camps – that somehow Interlink shareholders should somehow not be permitted to go about their business and if they happen to profit from that – well, it's just like Paul O'Neill said the other day about those energy guys: what you can do? It's the genius of capitalism.'

Suggestions that he is funding anything related to such un-Australian activities as people-smuggling are virulently denied. 'We are patriots!' he insists. Myers is quick to point out that Interlink are the largest single civilian contributor to research into new search-and-rescue radar systems for the Australian Navy ('We want to see Australia's borders defended, and there are thousands of miles of coastline where people who should, rightfully, end up in Woomera are slipping through the net') and also a generous donor to both Australian political parties. 'After all,' Myers points out earnestly, 'what could be healthier for political debate than providing funding to one political party that shares our values? Why, funding two such political parties!'

At the end of the day, however, Myers is careful to keep his feet on the ground and focused on the business at hand. 'We're proud of our role in helping defend this country's borders from the scourge of illegal immigration. We don't apologise for that. It isn't a popular thing, with the elites and what-have-you, but we are prepared to stand shoulder to shoulder with this Government to see the job done, whether that means supplying [the new camp in] Port Augusta with GLM or keeping up with a compounded growth year on year of between 15% and 25% in the number of people in camps, we'll be there.

'It's not just business,' Myers pauses, thinking, and then continues, 'It's about giving something back.'

The Chaser

shITe

Putting the WWW into wwwoeful, with shITemaster *Andrew Hansen*

Have a perfect life!

With the junk in your email inbox

LET 'shITe' **SHOW** you how to lead the perfect life!

That's right, all you need is an email account, and you can live in paradise!

Tired of how the other guy always has all the luck?

Feel like opening his jugular?

And bathing in the warm claret that spurts forth as the bastard goes down?

Why do some people float effortlessly over life's ocean while others struggle for air, smashed again and again by salty waves of misadventure?

Why are some people rich, secure, and happily married, while others battle like economic foot soldiers to pay the bills and eke out their blasted, lonely minutes on this wretched earth in a bare cell of an apartment, free from the solid laughter of love?

Only we at 'shITe' can tell you the secret to a **FLAWLESS EXISTENCE!**

And this is the secret.

The instructions leading to complete financial, emotional and sexual freedom are contained within your email Inbox.

YES! Instead of deleting the dozens of spam emails you receive each week, simply fall for their blatant tricks to get you to subscribe to their shabby newsletter, and take up all the sleazy offers they make!

Before long, you'll find you're no longer **DROWNING IN DEBT,** but will have saved up a bloated king's ransom by following the advice of people from other continents who specifically want you to become rich.

They're not dodgy 'pyramid' schemes, these junk emails. In fact, they are noble multi-level marketing schemes — wondrous, sophisticated plans that will see you showered with cash for little effort!

You'll be wealthy after pursuing just one of these offers ... so after following **ALL** of them, you'll be living beyond the sweatiest dreams of avarice!

What's more, once you've moved into your mansion, you can enjoy getting a **LEGAL** high every evening after sitting around all day not working. Simply toke away on the fully permissible cannabis substitutes you've obtained from the fine merchants in your junk email!

Meanwhile, for company, select from all the wonderful lovers you will have access to after investigating **EVERY** private dating service offered by your spam! Each service is extremely selective, and will provide only the most refined and caring people for you to begin a meaningful relationship with.

Then, entertain your many

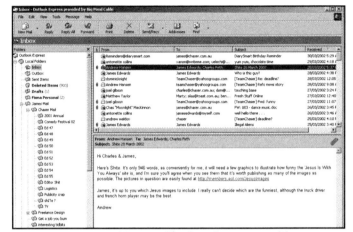

Email provides you with many life-changing opportunities

lovers with endless free pornography! Simply use your immense wealth and lack of debt to pay a membership fee to **ALL** the highly regarded **SEX** services that bombard you with emails.

They are truly superb!

And when it comes to showing off your **HOT BOD** to these paramours, you can come up with the goods ... and all because of your junk email!

That's right – simply keep ordering that Hunza diet bread, and within a few weeks you'll be slimmer and fitter. And remember to buy all those natural slimming pills online too! They are so healthy.

Life expectancy getting you down? Live twice as long with your junk email!

Use your credit card to buy life-lengthening foods and medicines, all from wholesome, trustworthy merchants.

And now that you are a 135-year-old stoned billionaire with the body of a Greek deity and a harem of lovers, why not enjoy your new, three-metre penis?

YES! You've received many email offers from companies claiming they can extend your penis by 30 cm or more.

The good news is, they **CAN** do just that!

But the **BEST** news is that if you buy the shorts-meat medicine and genital exercise charts from **ALL** of these reputable firms ... you'll build up a nob that's as long as a vacuum cleaner!

It's so useful and attractive.

Note: If enormous, serpentine penis too long to manage, simply coil around one ankle like a fire hose.

This feature brought to you courtesy of **shakeoffdebt296ds5 63kfjzncviowekfj@commail.ru**

Unsubscribe: Send an email to **autobounce927x@habaneros.br**

The Chaser

chase up ◆ HARASSMENT OF THE RICH AND FAMOUS ◆

This week, we discover that at 'Everything Here $2', things are not priced as they would seem...

```
TAX INVOICE

EVERYTHING HERE $2
Melbourne Central
Phone 9662-9622

ABN 33006122676

Description              Total
TAPE DISPENSER W/TAPE     0.67*
WRAP LOOSE A GOODMARK     0.50*
CDR 80MIN 700MB GAT SLIM CASE
      2 @ $1.25           2.50*

SubTotal                 $3.67

Rounding                -$0.02
-----------------------------
TOTAL (Inc GST)          $3.65
-----------------------------
4 Items

Cash Tendered           $20.00
Change Due              $16.35

GST Amount               $0.33

* Signifies item(s) with GST

Served by APRIL on lane 1

01/04/2002 15:39:13

3280101285637
```

The Manager
'Everything Here $2.00' Shop
Melbourne Central Shopping Centre
Swanston St, Melbourne 3000

Dear Sir or Madam,

RE: FALSE AND MISLEADING NAME OF SHOP

I visited your store, 'Everything here $2.00', this afternoon, where I purchased a number of sundry items. Though I was pleased by your extremely inexpensive prices, I regret that I didn't realize until later that all the items I purchased in fact cost less than $2.00. Indeed some of them cost less than half that. Being a person of integrity and fair dealing (unlike some I could name), I have included the $4.35 difference.

You are deliberately misleading consumers. I chose to shop with you not only because of your low prices, but because of their simplicity. In so many shops I am forced to carefully add up prices in order not to overstretch my budget. I thought your shop would be different. Well, you have failed me.

Frankly, I think a name change is in order. I would suggest: 'Some Things Here $2.00'. Although, let's face it, even that would be an exaggeration. Based on my experience, I think that 'Bloody well nothing here $2.00' would be more accurate. And if you're going to deliberately mislead the public, why not go the whole hog and call it 'Everything Here Free?'

Please be assured I will be informing the ACCC, not to mention the police, about your fraudulent behavior. I have some little familiarity with the Trade Practices Act, and I think that you may soon be forced to rename your shop 'Everything Here Closed Down'.

I will see you in court. And that, unlike the name of your store, is entirely sincere.

Regards,

Dominic Knight
The Chaser

www.chaser.com.au
Phone: (02) 9380 5051 Fax: (02) 9356 8591

Israel recruits NAB to close West Bank

TEL AVIV, Wednesday: Israeli security forces have successfully enlisted the expert help of the National Australia Bank to close down the West Bank. 'For years we'd been trying to shut down the West Bank, then Frank Cicutto comes along and manages to close the whole thing down in less than a week,' said a glowing Ariel Sharon.

The NAB's strategy relied on higher self-interest rates, a policy initially implemented by Sharon several months ago. Cicutto began his work in outlying villages of the West Bank. 'We're used to doing this stuff in regional areas,' explained Cicutto, as he completed the closure of all olive branches. The West Bank closure was eventually completed with a batch of new tank fees.

Cicutto expressed surprise at the common Israeli tactic of charging gunmen strongholds. 'For every gunman, there are another 20 ordinary citizens out there not being charged anything,' he said. 'Mortargage rates have been too low for too long.'

Cicutto denied that the NAB had only targeted Palestinians, pointing to the Troop Withdrawal fees that hit the Israel army hard in recent days. 'We've been totally fair, and anyway, if they have a complaint, they can always refer complaints to the Bombardsman.'

It only took days for Palestinians to flee the villages around the West Bank, surprising residents with the ease of its closure. 'Both my father and my grandfather died to save this land, and I had vowed to do the same,' said one Ramallah resident. 'But when the NAB presented me with the figures, and showed that it was just unsustainable – especially in view of what was happening in the US mortgage securitisation market – I couldn't help but accept their logic.'

National Australia Bank tanks move on a village outside Ramallah

Middle East at war: Melb paper struggles for Carey angle

Two attempts to link the earth-shattering news with the conflict in Israel

MELBOURNE, Monday: The editors of a leading Melbourne tabloid paper are struggling to find a Wayne Carey angle for their coverage of the escalating conflict in the Middle East.

The Murdoch-owned *Herald Sun* recently introduced an editorial policy stipulating that all news stories must contain at least one marketable tie-in to the disgraced AFL footballer.

Recent editions of the paper, for instance, have managed to link the Carey scandal to stories as diverse as NAB branch closures and stem cell research. But the editor admits it's been harder to cook up strong Carey leads on Israel's bombardment of Palestinian territory.

'We said Carey was in peace talks and covered his trip to Las Vegas discussing how he was safely out of harm's way from troop gunfire,' the editor said. 'And also a small piece on how Kellie Stevens is quite good friends with a Jew, whose family originally hailed from Israel.'

The editor said the paper also published a comparison story on the fact that both Israel and Wayne Carey had at various times invaded other people's territory. 'And both were told to withdraw when their respective occupations were exposed,' he said.

Tomorrow will mark the fortieth consecutive day the *Herald Sun* will have covered the Carey story in one form or another. The paper is celebrating this by promoting the story to the front page.

Real estate agent describes Ramallah property as 'renovator's delight'

WEST BANK, Wednesday: A 34-year-old West Bank real estate agent has enjoyed incredible success since the recent surge in hostilities between Palestine and Israel.

'I don't understand why everyone's bitching so much around here,' Kuma Rakat told reporters. 'In my experience, land has never been so much in demand. You wouldn't believe the price the Israeli government was willing to pay for some of my Gaza Strip listings.'

Rakat believes the protracted laying waste of his homeland has added value to many of his Ramallah properties.

'I have this one great property right near Yasser's place – a real renovator's delight. Well ventilated, skylight recently installed, breathtaking views and conveniently located right where the action is – I've got potential buyers beating down the door for this one.'

Rakat is particularly complimentary about Israel's provision of a regular, efficient transportation truck from the West Bank to a wide variety of prisons and secret interrogation rooms, describing public transport as 'a real seller'.

'The Israeli Government's mindless and random attacks are just what our economy needed,' concluded Rakat. 'Now these are boom times.'

Keen masturbator spikes own drink with Rohypnol

SYDNEY, Friday: A man describing himself as a passionate masturbator has admitted that he spiked his own drink with the drug Rohypnol in order to have his way with himself.

The man told police he deliberately set out to prey on his own company, by slipping the potent sedative pill into his vodka and tonic while he wasn't looking. He said his plan from the outset was to take advantage of himself while his defences were down.

'I was really on the hunt for some self-abuse,' the man said. 'And when I saw this hottie bit of hand leaning on the bar I slipped myself a mickey, and the next thing I know I was taking myself back to my place.'

Police have described the man as one of several predatory masturbators currently operating in watering holes around the inner city of Sydney. 'In fact, it's fair to say that most Sydney bars are full of wankers,' a police spokesman said.

Passionate masturbator on the prowl

Andrew Weldon

The Chaser

Pope desperate for sainthood: Claims his incontinence a miracle

VATICAN, Tuesday: Pope John Paul II this week claimed he had achieved several miracles in a last ditch attempt to achieve sainthood. The week climaxed yesterday when the Pope claimed that a wet patch left by his incontinence was a miracle.

'It was a wonder to see, one moment his robes were white and then suddenly they became yellow,' said a Papal aide. 'The fact that the wet patch was in the shape of the Virgin Mary only confirmed that it was a miracle.'

The Pope also claimed several other miracles during the week, including remaining awake through an entire Easter service and keeping down his breakfast on Thursday. The Pope,

The aging Pope tried to miraculously string two sentences together

present at the press conference, did not speak to gathered media, but dozed next to the podium.

Some Papal observers have questioned several of

the claimed miracles. 'I'm pretty sure that that stigmata the Pope showed us last week was just a bed sore,' said one.

So far the Committee for

Beatification has only accepted one of the Pope's claimed miracles as completely legitimate: his success in surviving the Queen Mother.

Nobel laureates queue to pitch life stories to Hollywood

LOS ANGELES, Friday: Hollywood studios have been inundated by a rash of Nobel laureates eager to pitch movies based on their lives, in the wake of the recent successful biopic *A Beautiful Mind*.

Laureates from fields as diverse as chemistry and literature now understand that the major studios want to make movies about the lives of prize-winning academics.

'I always thought my life

researching lepton physics would make a good film,' said 1995 laureate Frederick Reines. 'But it wasn't until I saw that John Nash movie clean up at the Oscars that I got the confidence to finally make an appointment with Paramount.'

Dr Reines told studio executives over a short lunch that he thought film audiences were ready for a film about his long career hunched over data in the University of

California physics laboratory. 'I pitched it as a light romantic comedy,' he said. 'Obviously you'd take my discovery of the tau lepton as the starting point, and then develop a series of humorous complications leading up to my research team's breakthrough detection of the neutrino.'

Another esteemed laureate, Ronald H. Coase, who was awarded the Nobel Prize for Economics, said he's very

keen to arrange a meeting with Miramax to discuss the prospect of developing a feature about his award-winning research project into the significance of transaction costs and property rights for institutional economic structures.

'I told them I thought Tom Hanks would be perfect in the role of me,' Dr Coase said. 'They said they'd get back to me on it. And that was about three months ago.'

Saddam equips Iraq with nuclear weapons: running water next

BAGHDAD, Friday: Iraqi president Saddam Hussein has promised to have his country fully armed with nuclear weapons in one year's time, a spending commitment which he described as Iraq's number one priority over other services such as medicine or running water. President Hussein said he wouldn't turn his attention to 'secondary, less vital luxuries' such as a basic water supply until he was satisfied the country was adequately equipped for full-scale nuclear warfare.

US Defense officials are concerned that the sanctions which they've imposed on Iraq have done nothing to prevent the country's ability to rebuild its nuclear capabilities. They're equally worried that the same sanctions will now allow the country's civilians to access basic services like water.

Defense strategists fear running water could strengthen President Hussein's grip on power by removing any reason for Iraqi dissidents to revolt against the brutal military dictatorship.

Officials are so concerned by Iraq's progress they have put the 'water threat' at the top of a list of the top ten risks to global security. Other factors on the list include the threat North Korea may produce enough rice to feed its population within a decade and the risk that India may build more pharmaceuticals factories to supply patented AIDS drugs to poor countries.

Saddam is almost as excited about the water as the nukes he ordered

Dave: really good busker

Tourist mistakes statue of David for motionless busker

FLORENCE, Tuesday: An American tourist visiting Italy yesterday mistook the renowned statue of David for a stationary busker. The man stood watching Michaelangelo's masterpiece for more than ten minutes, transfixed by how still it managed to keep.

'I've seen a lot of these buskers around the world, and this was definitely one of the better ones,' the tourist said. 'I swear – I didn't see it move once. In fact, I was so impressed I threw him a few lira.'

The man said he wasn't sure where to place the 1000 lira note, given the busker had modestly neglected to put out a hat. 'I ended up putting it inside this slingshot purse thingy he seemed to be carrying,' he said. 'And even with me climbing up on him to squeeze it in, he didn't so much as blink! I mean, this guy was good.'

The American tourist said the only fault he could find with the busker was aesthetic. 'The actual design and sculpting of his costume was a bit amateur,' he said. 'I mean, I've seen much more intricate statue suits back home in the States. There's this big woman who holds a torch on Ellis Island in New York who's particularly realistic.'

The Chaser

Saint Bono preaches from his pulpit

Bono satisfies world hunger for preachy rock stars

DUBLIN, Thursday: U2's lead singer Bono has launched a daring solo mission to end the world's hunger for rock stars who use their high profiles to crap on self-righteously about charitable causes. After appointing himself planetary spokesman for poor people, Bono has dedicated himself to the cause through simplistic half-hour lectures on charity. While his only contribution to the world has been to make himself and multinational record companies fabulously wealthy, Bono is reported to believe the lectures will somehow end world famine.

'For many years, my people and I have felt ignored,' said Eric Mbeke, 13, of Ethiopia, with what later proved to be his last breaths. 'But now that Bono has taken up our cause, we know that not everyone is ignoring us, just the people who are in a position to do something about it.'

The U2 singer says his motivation is simple – to live up to his name. 'I call myself "Bono", which means "good" – but how good am I really if there's someone out there who doesn't have enough to eat?' he asked. But while many have dismissed his efforts as tokenistic, the respected anti-famine group Oxfam has applauded Bono's halting of his touring commitments to lobby world leaders. 'Bono's efforts have touched people all over the world,' a spokesperson said. 'The cancelling of U2 concerts is only a small step towards making the world a better place, but you'd have to admit it's a great start.'

US stock market ends on record low: Trader ends night on record high

NEW YORK: Wall Street records tumbled yesterday after a fall in tech stocks and a record cocaine binge by Ricky Johnson of Merrill Lynch. Both records rattled spectators who witnessed them unfolding.

'It was scary to watch. First the NASDAQ lost 420 points and then Ricky lost about 5 grand at the club after work,' said Kenneth Williams of Schroeders.

Many small time traders and investors were harmed by the fall in the tech market having believed that it had bounced back since a post-September 11 slump.

Several small time traders were also harmed by Ricky's cocaine-induced obnoxiousness.

'He told Eddie Kimpson that he couldn't trade his way out of his shithouse Queens apartment and then told him that his wife was fucking uglier than his arse,' said Williams. 'Eddie nearly cried.'

Several waitresses also suffered at the hands of Ricky. Both the NASDAQ and Ricky had poor rebounds the next day, ending the day very low.

Ricky Johnson: record high

The Chaser

How to fool people into thinking you're

A Stiff, Reliable Chaser How-To Guide™

A Howard family as an optional extra, easily fashioned out of cardboard or thin plywood if required

Dear *Chaser Annual* reader, in the last few weeks alone, over 1,000 people have taken advantage of an unprecedented opportunity exclusive to *The Chaser Annual*!

Elite Members: We wanted to give *The Chaser Annual* Elite Members ONE MORE CHANCE to get involved before we went public and made this offer available to all the dozens of people who read *The Chaser* the rest of the time.

It took some begging, but thankfully the editors agreed to put off the public release for ONE MORE WEEK!

If you're unfamiliar with what this is about, read on. It's incredible.

A very prominent and successful businessman out of Seattle, Washington by the name of Andrew Hansen has decided to split the power with you 50-50 on very lucrative deals using a very simple Technique™ that sinister government people are trying to keep very secret.

Not only is it realistic to become the RULER of the WHOLE OF AUSTRALIA using Mr Hansen's Technique™, Mr Hansen takes ALL the risk away from you

by PROVIDING ALL THE MONEY needed for YOU to complete highly profitable procedures!

(Legal disclaimer: No money is needed to complete these highly profitable procedures.)

Put simply: to assume SUPREME COMMAND OF ALL AUSTRALIA, you must become the Prime Minister.

Sound tricky? Don't worry! You CAN be Prime Minister without winning ANY complicated elections or ascending to the pinnacle of ANY distinguished political career!

First, take a good look at our real Prime Minister, or 'PM', Mr John Howard. Now, make some flesh-coloured dough, and apply it to your face in such a way as to simulate the doughy lines and bumps on Howard's own amusing little face.

Strip the fur from two rats, and squeeze the matted tufts into the dough above your eyes to form distinguished eyebrows.

And so on. In fact, John Howard has been caricatured so many times already, there's no need for us to do it here! Nor so badly, either.

Now, you will need a building from which to conduct your supreme reign – that's right, a Parliament House!

Have a good look at the existing Parliament House. It's in Canberra. Now, you'll need an architect. Ask all of your friends if they know any architects, and when you've tracked one down, offer to take him or her to lunch in Canberra, in the Parliament House restaurant.

Over lunch, nonchalantly work into the conversation that you wish to build an exact replica of Parliament House.

Insist that your architect

The Chaser

draw you a full wad of plans for constructing a new Parliament House, identical to the present one. If the architect frowns and declines your offer with a frightened look in their eyes, searching the room for the waiter in order to pay the bill and leave the restaurant, simply produce some bent nails and use them to rip the architect's small, tender nostrils until he or she accedes, quaking with fear.

Now, use a tractor to clear a block of land somewhere close to the current Parliament House, in Manuka or somewhere like that.

Using bricks and paint and other building materials, construct a full-sized replica of Parliament House on your block of land. This will be your seat of glory! And all this time, YOU will look exactly like John Howard as you toil in the harsh Australian weather to build your palace of democracy.

Now, using a screwdriver and pliers, drive around Canberra, and wherever you see a road sign directing people to Parliament House,

twist it around so it points towards your own Parliament House.

Soon your Parliament House will fill up with Members of Parliament, duped by your road signs into changing their workplace, as well as unwitting tourists from all over the world!

Worried about what happens when the REAL John Howard walks in? Easy!

Simply cause a spectacular scene, accusing the man of being an impostor. Then rip off his eyebrows and doughy clumps of his face as if they were false items of makeup.

Note: You may need to rip very hard, as Mr Howard wears real brows and face-clumps.

Within minutes, the police, tricked by your skilful bluff, will apprehend Mr Howard, leaving you free to claim his throne!

All you need to do now is continue to pretend you are the all-powerful Prime Minister, and go to Parliamentary sittings and things, and be a reactionary fucker.

ALL HAIL YOU, PRIME MINISTER SUPREME, UNDISPUTED RULER OF ALL AUSTRALIA.

This student wondered whether her prom ensemble was appropriate

Woman still ugly after removing glasses

LOS ANGELES, Sunday: A plain-looking high school student was last night mortified at her end-of-year prom to discover that she didn't transform into a stunning beauty after taking off her glasses.

The young woman had been led to believe by Hollywood movies that she would instantly bloom into a ravishing young woman simply by removing her spectacles. But instead she

was revealed to be just as unattractive as she was before.

The student's humiliation was increased by the fact that she cast off her frames while dancing with the school's handsome and popular school captain. She was expecting he would be struck speechless by her transformation, and be forced to immediately re-evaluate his indifferent opinion of her, but instead he merely reaffirmed his view that she was a boring, ugly dag.

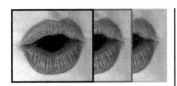

spit *or* swallow?

An advice column for the modern era.

Dear Spit,

Days have passed without my friends calling me. Realising no one cared about me, I plotted my own massacre: at 2 a.m. on a Saturday I walked down dark alleys yelling provocative abuse in order to get killed and obtain friends' sympathy. However, not even a murderer wants me. Why?

Geraldine Coastal

Dear Geraldine,

Obviously you are so boring you have disappeared from this world and into the limbo of your imagination. Sometimes humans are too thick to realise how tedious the rest of society finds them.

Dear Spit,

I had a terrible mouse plague in my apartment, so I hired a pest control man to set traps and kill the rodents. The pest man laid these odd sticky traps that the mice are supposed to stick to and die. However in a moment of madness I placed my penis on the gooey trap, and now it's stuck.

James Re Weed

Dear James,

Either rip your dick off the trap and risk losing all penile feeling, or leave the trap on and experience the pleasure of mice nibbling at your foreskin. These traps were originally built as a sex aid, but were phased out when couples returned to the simple art of feathering.

Pope demands abortion of cloned child

Pope: ensures 'job done right'

VATICAN, Monday: The Vatican has condemned a woman who has been impregnated with a clone of her husband and called for immediate action.

However the church is unsure what course of action should be taken. 'On the one hand, we think there is no way that this unnatural child can be born into God's world – and therefore it should be aborted immediately,' said a spokesperson for the Pope. 'On the other hand, there is no way this woman should be allowed to abort her child.'

The Pope has reportedly agonised over how to prevent the birth of the child without preventing the birth of the child. The quandary has appeared particularly tough to solve while retaining the Pope's trademark hypocrisy.

'Luckily for the Pope,' continued the spokesman, 'He does have a bit of leeway on the issue, being infallible and all.'

The dilemma has come at a particularly bad time for the Pope, who is suffering from Parkinson's disease. The dementia prevents him from making rational decisions, a condition which has resulted in obvious effects since the release of his encyclical *Humanae Vitae* in 1968.

Complicating the decision further are recent claims that a cloned human may suffer from the same symptoms as the first cloned sheep – notably arthritis, premature aging and a thick coat of wool.

Other Christian denominations have already come out in favour of human cloning. Priests in the Brisbane diocese of the Anglican Church have particularly shown an interest in the cloning of defenceless 14-year-old girls.

The Chaser

Banner writers miss Waugh brothers: Struggle to make pun out of 'Hayden'

JOHANNESBURG, Monday: Cricket supporters across the nation have bemoaned the loss of Australian wordplay's greatest servants, the Waugh brothers.

Their departure is the latest in a long line of bitter disappointments for banner writers following the recent retirements of Paul Reiffel and Tom Moody.

'The selectors have got it completely wrong,' said Bill Gibson, an irate fan. 'Ten years ago there were banners that read "You broke the LAW when you crossed our BORDER. Now you MAY need HEALYing cause we're MOODY and declaring a TAYLOR-made WAUGH with our REIFFEL". But these days the selectors have buggered everything up.'

Gibson cited the name 'Hayden' as a particular concern, calling for Hayden's immediate dismissal from the team regardless of his test average of 50. His appeal comes after trialling banners 'Send them to HAYDENes', 'South Africa have the chance of a needle in a HAYDENstack' and 'It's back to our HAYDENday' to little acclaim.

'But it doesn't end there,' added Gibson. 'Just look at the guy who replaced Waugh – Lehmann. The only banner I've seen about him is "Just LEHMIN' around". Now, what the fuck's that? It doesn't even make sense.'

Banner writers have faced challenges before, most notably from Michael Kasprowicz's inclusion in the side, only to rise to the occasion with the now much-loved standard 'KASPROWICKETS'.

'Yeah we can still go into bat with a "Love-LEE" or a "You've been WARNED",' admitted Gibson. 'But the new players don't have the same versatility. With the name "Waugh" you can choose "Man-o-WAUGH", "WAUGH on two fronts" or the simple elegance of "WAUGH zone". I guess the selectors have just gotten a little WAUGH-weary.'

World awaits Iraq Wars II: Attack of the Clone

WASHINGTON, Tuesday: Audiences around the world are eagerly waiting in anticipation of the release of the *Iraq Wars* sequel, *Iraq Wars II: Attack of the Clone*.

The production's all star cast includes President George W. Bush who plays the direct clone of former President George Bush from *Iraq Wars I*. Several other stars from *Iraq Wars I* have returned for the sequel, including Dick Cheney and Colin Powell.

'The special effects on this one are amazing,' said Powell who plays the dove interest in the new movie. 'I can hardly tell the difference between the Bushes when it comes to invading Iraq. Although I guess the first Bush was actually provoked a bit.'

The anticipated release has seen enormous profits from merchandising with huge sales of American flags leading the way. Merchandisers in the arms manufacturing industry are also reporting strong sales in the lead up to the sequel.

American audiences in particular have been keen to see the start of the sequel, with many calling for it to be released early. In Britain movie-goers have been less keen, suggesting that they will attend the sequel now that it's going ahead, but would have preferred that there had not been a follow-up to the first blockbuster.

The *Iraq Wars* sequel is also eagerly awaited in Australia. Many Australians have played minor roles in the production of the sequel including Prime Minister John Howard.

IRAQ WARS

EPISODE II

ATTACK OF THE CLONE

Parasite labels Harmer
its worst host ever

Costello promises Medibank sell-off won't interfere with rising premiums

CANBERRA, Friday: Treasurer Peter Costello has assured the public that his proposed sell-off of Medibank Private will in no way compromise the insurance giant's systematic contempt for its members.

'Not only do I guarantee that premiums will continue to skyrocket if Medibank is privatised, but I expect it to require as many, if not more, embarrassing bail-outs from the government,' said Costello. 'And that's an iron-clad guarantee.'

Consumer advocates had earlier expressed concerns about the effect of the decision on rural Australia. However, Costello reassured them with an undertaking that no sale would be contemplated unless he was completely satisfied rural Australians would retain the scandalously poor medical coverage they currently enjoy.

In the past Medibank was seen as a crucial link between the Government and the health insurance industry but Costello declared that an outdated view, 'I would have thought the sizeable Liberal Party donations made by health insurance companies provided a more than adequate link between us,' he said.

Medibank Private, to be renamed Medibank Public upon privatisation, could potentially fetch as much as $1 billion for the Government, money which Costello described as a vital injection to the Government's fund for rescuing newly privatised companies.

'Medibank has lost over $50 million in the past few months,' explained Costello

Costello: privatising to fund bail-outs

in justifying the sale. 'Surely its balance sheet alone proves it's ready to take its place among Australia's privately-owned insurance giants.'

Ruddock slams media focus on refugees: 'Nobody mentions my mishandling of Abos'

CANBERRA, Tuesday: Minister for Immigration and Indigenous Affairs Phillip Ruddock has lashed out against the Australian media's 'constant criticism' of the government's refugee policies, claiming his 'equally mis-guided' indigenous policies were not getting the attention they deserved.

Speaking to a gathering of Pakistani officials in Islamabad, Mr Ruddock voiced his concerns about the biased reporting of his Department's activities.

'I have fought long and hard to bring the same commitment to a White Australia to both my portfolio responsibilities', he said. 'I have used the same right-wing notions of individual responsibility, the same inferences of blame and the same stubborn inability to listen in the running of Indigenous Affairs as I have in Immigration. But what gets the most attention? The illegal immigrants.'

Ruddock said he hoped that the media would mature.

'One day it will be intelligent enough to cover our own, home-grown oppression rather than have to look for foreign victims.'

Ruddock: focussing on home-grown oppression

The Chaser

Psychiatric patient successfully reintegrated into homeless community

MELBOURNE, Tuesday: Australia's mental institutions have achieved an almost 100% success rate in their program to reintegrate patients back into the homeless community. The news comes as a relief to psychiatric support groups who were concerned about the effect increased funding cuts were having on psychiatric care.

'With relatively little assistance, most patients have fitted in with the vagrant population that wanders the city,' said Kenmore mental institution CEO Jennifer Carson.

Carson claims that the speed with which mental patients can be returned to the streets is a consequence of years of de-institutionalisation.

'We now have so many former patients on the street that new patients really get a leg up in the homeless community,' said Carson. 'Finding the right doorways and soup kitchens on their own can be hard for mental retards.'

The government has pointed to the new figures in response to attacks against their policies which have seen beds in mental institutions fall by 60% in the last ten years.

'The streets are preferable

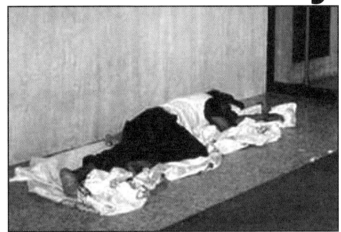
Another success story for the reintegration program

because they are cheaper,' said Health Minister Kay Paterson. 'But don't worry, the patients still receive the same abuse and neglect that they experienced in mental institutions.'

Couple hires Glenn Murcutt to design their designer baby

MELBOURNE, Tuesday: A Melbourne couple has contracted the award-winning Australian architect Glenn Murcutt to design their designer baby.

The style-conscious couple said they'd approached a number of leading world designers, from Frank Gehry to Terence Conran, before agreeing to award the contract for their child's genes to Murcutt.

'More than anyone else, he understood the brief at once,' explained the expecting mother. 'I mean, people like Seidler kept telling us we should build the child as big as possible. But it would have been an eyesore. Whereas Glenn seemed to grasp that we wanted something elegant but natural – something that would sit harmoniously with its environment.'

Murcutt's preliminary designs for the child involve the use of natural corrugated iron. 'I love using simple, raw materials,' Murcutt said. 'And if I can evoke the classic Australian wool shed in this child's torso and limbs, then I think we'll have a really unique infant with loads of natural light.'

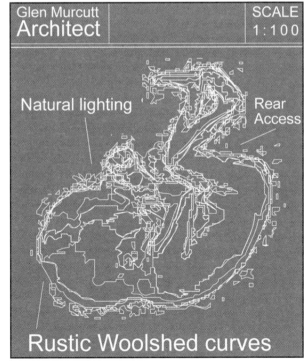

Glen Murcutt
Architect
SCALE 1:100
Natural lighting
Rear Access
Rustic Woolshed curves

Murcutt's early drafts for the baby

Newlyweds: did not expect such violence

Tarantino reduced to doing wedding videos

LOS ANGELES, Saturday: Former Hollywood golden boy Quentin Tarantino has hit such a career rut that he's been forced to shoot wedding videos just to make ends meet.

The once critically acclaimed director has been filming weddings and corporate videos for the past two months, hoping to recapture the spark which a few years ago made him the industry's hottest young film-maker.

A couple who recently hired Tarantino for their wedding day said they found him very difficult to work with. They recalled growing nervous as production on the wedding blew right out, putting them well behind schedule and over budget.

'Let's just say it wasn't the fairytale wedding we'd dreamed of,' the groom confided. 'For a start, there was a lot of unnecessary violence which Quentin insisted on putting in. In fact, by the time we signed

the registry most of the congregation had either been shot dead, or locked in a basement with a gimp.'

The groom also remembered most of the service was rewritten by Tarantino, so that every second prayer was in black ghetto slang and included the word 'motherfucker'. More controversial still was the director's decision to cast John Travolta in a cameo as the organist.

When the couple finally viewed the finished product, they were baffled to discover the director had played around with the chronology of their wedding.

'The film actually started at the reception,' the distraught newlyweds said. 'It then cut back to our vows, skipped ahead to the cutting of the cake and finished with the bride walking down the aisle.'

The couple nonetheless said they did quite enjoy the scene where the best man cut off the marriage celebrant's ear.

Burmese regime makes genuine commitment to pretence of change

RANGOON, Monday: The government of Myanmar (Burma) released democratic opposition leader Aung San Suu Kyi today after a year and a half of house arrest. Her release is a major part of the government's radical new program of changing Burma's political system to make it superficially seem less authoritarian. The spokesman for the military junta that rules the nation, Lieutenant Colonel Hla Min, said that the move was a 'new page' for Burma, although he later clarified that he meant a new page in a work of fiction.

'Aung San Suu Kyi is now free to do anything she wishes in relation to her party's activities,' Min said. 'As her party is banned, of course, that means she is free to do nothing.' The government expects that Aung San Suu Kyi will conduct meetings with supporters, hold a number of restrained demonstrations and, most importantly, convince the West to give Burma the

millions of dollars of aid it withheld while she was under house arrest. 'Make no mistake, Suu Kyi's release will change things enormously for this country's current rulers,' Min said. 'Our bank balances will increase substantially.'

Suu Kyi made a triumphant return to the headquarters of her National League of Democracy party today, where she vowed to continue her fight for genuine democracy in the Asian state. For its part, the ruling group has agreed to keep advancing the process of appearing to change. 'We have already shown we can achieve fundamental change in Myanmar,' Min said. 'A few years ago, we in the ruling military committee changed our name from the State Law and Order Reform Committee to the State Peace and Development Council. This is exactly the kind of far-reaching, visionary change you will see from us as we continue to make Myanmar seem more democratic.'

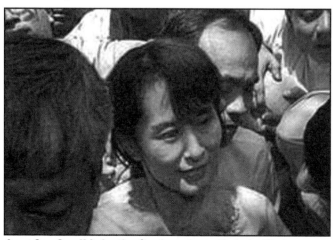

Aung San Suu Kyi shortly after her release that signified a new pretence of progress

The Chaser

RADIO FREQUENCY

Industry rumour has it that on 30 June this year, an undisclosed Australian commercial radio station will make history by broadcasting a different song.

It is the talk of DJs and programmers around the nation.

Whichever station will pull the unprecedented, daring stunt is unknown. But pamphlets have been distributed in mailboxes nationwide claiming that on 30 June, commercial radio listeners will actually hear a song that isn't on the station's daily playlist.

'It's ridiculous,' says Triple M Sydney's programming director [name withheld]. 'It'll never work.

'In all my years in commercial radio, nothing like this has been tried before.

Nova: really, like, diverse

Therefore it won't work.

'Nobody wants to hear stuff other than the 50 or so fixed songs that the major record companies instruct us to broadcast over and over and over again every day without change. Everyone knows that.'

The feeling in the radio industry is that the 'different' song to be aired once only on 30 June – a date now being referred to as 'Playlist D-Day' – will be an extremely obscure piece of music. It may even be another track from an album by an already playlisted artist other than the appointed radio single from that same album.

Therefore the 'different' song could be something as weird as, for example, a track from Weezer's album Weezer other than 'Island in the Sun'!

'Awwwwwwwwwww,' comments Nova FM's DJ Bianca. 'That's a fully shiddouse ideeaah!

'I can't believe any station would go that far. All the listeners will fully turn off the second they hear it, I swear.

'Whichever station's doing this it's certainly not us at Nova. We know what's a good song and we stick to it.

'Then we never let go.

'Anyway our playlist is heaps diverse already, there must be dozens of hit songs we play. We don't bore people with other shiddouse songs.'

Government station Triple J's programming director [name withheld] is similarly sceptical.

'Here at Triple J, we can afford to be eclectic and experimental, often playing as many as two different songs a month.

'But for a radio station to be popular, it really can't afford to introduce naïve things like creativity and imagination into its operation.

'People want to hear music they already know – that's the best kind of music.

'Mind you, I'm not sure how people first get to know the music they already know. But that's never been radio's concern.

'It's like those funny bands that play in pubs, making up their own songs. The only people who go to see them are people in other bands who make up their own songs.

'What we all want is a good band. A band who knows how to play good music, like "American Pie" by Elton John. Or "November Rain" by Belinda Carlisle.

'Ooh what a giveaway. I love Triple J. It is very fresh.'

Andrew Weldon

Celebrity advice

With special guest
Labor's policy thug
Mark Latham

Q: I suffer from cerebral palsy which has left me wheelchair-bound. I find it difficult to form romantic attachments to women as they don't see past the wheelchair. What can I do to show them the real me?

A: **You can start by standing up for yourself and not being such a spastic about it. I'm not criticising you for being a spastic in terms of being afflicted by a chronic condition in which your muscles are affected by persistent spasms because of damage to motor nerves. But what I do believe is that you are a complete spastic in terms of your character, afflicted by a chronic condition in which you are disabled from being proactive romantically because you lack the nerve to muscle up to women. That's all I'm saying.**

Q: What are the key policy issues that the Labor Party will be campaigning on during 2002?

A: **Do you think in the Labor Party we're just a doormat for the likes of Abbott and Staley and Howard to challenge us on matters of policy? I am interested in challenging the Liberals on character and behaviour, that's clear from the context of the debate on Friday night. If any other inference has been taken then I'm sorry for that.**

Q: A man I dated over a year ago has continued to call me even though I have asked him to desist. Now he hangs around outside my house and threatens to kill my dogs. What should I do to make him stop?

A: **That may be the case but I'll tell you something right now: any harassment you may be facing pales into insignificance when you consider the disgraceful campaign run by the Liberal Party against Paul Keating as a private citizen. We're talking about Paul Keating's private affairs, three years out of politics. Think about that and then I might give some thought to your question.**

Q: I have ambitions to lead the Labor Party. Can you suggest a way for me to differentiate myself?

A: **Try becoming a campaigner against anatomical incorrectness.**

Sports Comment
with Harold Parkes

Time for Webber to score a couple in the pits

These days, Australians are the only thing more rare in Formula One racing than tall blokes with beards and ugly sheilas.

Bravo Mark Webber, whose emergence from the burgeoning ranks of our young go-kart and slot car champions to take 5th place in Jeffrey Kennett's race last weekend was a welcome surprise.

No surprise, however, to learn that he was conceived and taught to drive in Queanbeyan, a town where there is little to do besides conceive young men and teach them how to drive.

A short hock and spit away lies the national capital, where Webber no doubt honed his skills on those long, straight roads away from the watchful eyes of mum, dad, police patrol cars and red light cameras.

Having collected two valuable points for his Minardi team, thanks in part to the early exit of nine other drivers, young Webber now knows what it is to stand in the inner circle of F1 drivers.

The time has come, then, for the man they call 'Queen Bee' to take his prize.

It's no secret that Formula One is every virile sportsman's wet dream, and not simply for the money on offer. Pete Sampras is as rich a man as Edward Irvine, but he smiles a lot less.

Those who call Greg Norman 'The Shark' never saw Alain Prost on his days off.

I did, however. Webber is now in a position to become Australia's most highly sexed professional athlete. He has the opportunity to emulate Queanbeyan's other favourite son, David 'Too Easy' Campese, and root his way around the globe for as long as he fits into his helmet and leathers.

Let me assure you, the number of tries Campo scored during his career paled in comparison to the number of shots he put between the sticks. And all in spite of a much-documented weakness in the tackle.

Sources tell me that Webber's performance in practice and qualifying so far has left much to be desired, that he has allowed state-of-the-art equipment to be wasted by the rashness of youth. Not yet accustomed to performing at this level, we can forgive the lad a few early stutters. A slow lap time, complications with a drive shaft or a head gasket, being overtaken on the inside. These are errors to be expected from one so raw.

To cement his position, Webber knows what lies ahead. If he fails, there is no shortage of other young hopefuls waiting in the wings, primed and pumped but without two Pennys to rub together.

Eight easy ways to

I'm just about sick of this Middle East crisis. For goodness' sakes, people. Unless you manage to completely eradicate the other race – and I'll have to admit, you're doing a bang-up job so far – you're going to have to come up with a solution eventually. And while every attempt so far has been marred by failure, there is one person who is so far untested, but clearly has an excellent chance of coming up with a workable, lasting, mutually beneficial solution to the crisis. Me. Therefore I present not one, but eight, solutions to the crisis. Now, you don't have to thank me. I will receive enough thanks if there's an end to all the killing. Though a Nobel Peace Prize would be nice, and, I think, entirely appropriate.

1) Find a common enemy

In many cases, conflicts are solved when the parties realise that the things that unite them are greater than the things that divide them. Obviously whatever unites Israel and Palestine is going to have to be pretty bloody big. Which is why they should gang together and invade Iraq. It'd be fun, easy and the Americans would probably even pay for it. It's an unprecedented bonding opportunity – even Iran would probably join in for old times' sake.

2) Find Jesus

Religion is the main cause of their division, and we can hardly expect the Palestinians to convert to Judaism. The rules say you have to be turned away twice first, and the Palestinians don't exactly have a strong reputation for patience. Nor are the Israelis likely to convert to Islam – they'd all have to cut off their hands for stealing the Occupied Territories. So the solution is clearly for them both to convert to a neutral religion such as Christianity – I'm thinking of the Pentecostal 'let's all sing and fall over with the joy of the spirit' variety. I can just see Sharon and Arafat joining hands and singing 'Amazing Grace'.

Alternatively, if they won't renounce their own religions, they could actually find Jesus. As Jews and Muslims, they don't buy the resurrection theory, so his remains ought to be kicking around in a tomb somewhere. If they do find him, they could give a bit of him to that strange Italian scientist for cloning. It might finally shut Christians up about the Second Coming.

3) Consumerism

Why do the vast majority of us enlightened Westerners no longer endlessly fight pointless wars based on race and religion? It's very simple. First there's the overwhelming desire not to be like the Irish, and then there's the enormous practical problem – there isn't enough time thanks to the endless delight of consumer products. Would young Palestinians really go and blow themselves up in the middle of Israel if they knew they'd be leaving behind an unfinished PlayStation 2 game, or before the Harry Potter series is finished? And would Israel be intent on killing Palestinians if they thought of them all as customers for their burgeoning software industry? This is the real failing of America in the Middle East – to ensure sufficient penetration of their consumerist culture and lifestyle to make the locals pliant, passive and content, just like the rest of us.

4) Sharon and Arafat should finally sleep together

You'd have to say there's a bit of tension in their relationship. Ariel and Yasser have been fighting for decades like Han Solo and Princess Leia in the first two Star Wars movies. It's definitely time they got down to the pay-off we all know is coming. Plus, I think they'd make a cute couple. Ariel clearly has a tender side – he's named after a famous book of poetry by Sylvia Plath, and Sharon isn't exactly the most macho name either. I'm sure that the love of an honest Palestinian ex-terrorist with an overfondness for headscarves is just what he needs to make him happy and fulfilled, rather than so very angry all the time.

5) Denigrate other Middle Eastern countries

The denigration of others is the social glue that brings people together – just ask Jean-Marie Le Pen's voters. In high school, people in the 'cool group' often make fun of others to cement their own insecure bonds. Arafat and Sharon need to do the same thing, perhaps with the help of some nicknames that only they use? If both of them began referring to Jordan as 'Bore-dan', for instance, they'd be able to laugh together at that rather dull kingdom. And that's not all. 'Saudi Arabia' could become 'Dowdy Arabia', and they could dub 'Iran' 'I-also-ran' – think of the fun they'd have! I would also like to go on the public record and say that if it will help the peace process, they are welcome to use these nicknames I've devised.

The Chaser

Middle East peace

6) Take up hobbies

Hobbies are a great way of relaxing and also spending time with those who share your interests. While one would have to commend the craft skills of the young Palestinians who construct homemade bombs and explode themselves, it's not the most soothing hobby they could have. Part of the problem is that tried-and-true Western hobbies such as quilting and knitting are fairly inappropriate given the prevailing climate in this part of the world. But with the right approach from the government, we may one day see people disinclined to fight because they're absorbed in their stamp collections. Who knows – one day Israelis and Palestinians may even trade stamps with one another. And that's a vision worth working towards.

Ariel and Yasser get a piece for peace

7) Smoke drugs together

I think it's safe to say from the present levels of anger flowing through the region that not nearly enough ganja has gone down there lately. A Cypress Hill tour would be a great start, and George W. Bush – no stranger to the allure of chemicals himself – should probably also appoint Woody Harrelson as a special Presidential envoy. Then we'd see Ariel and Yasser smoking a peace pipe, and confessing their love for one another (see #4). This plan is not without its flaws, however, as there is a shortage of the necessary support services. Dial-A-Pizza is still not readily available within the Occupied Territories.

8) Mutually assured destruction

Giving both sides of a conflict an awesome nuclear arsenal is actually the only 100% proven method of obtaining peace in a hurry. The lack of a nuclear war during the Reagan presidency also illustrates that it's absolutely foolproof. We're already halfway there, as Israel already has nukes. (And it's absolutely amazing Sharon hasn't used them yet, given his reputation for restraint.) But if the Palestinian youth in the crowded Jerusalem café had a gigantic nuclear warhead strapped to himself, and there was absolute certainty that he'd destroy the whole of Palestine as well as Israel, then surely there is a chance (albeit very small) he'd think twice before setting it off.

So there you have it. Solving the Middle East crisis wasn't that hard, was it? Now bring on the Irish, I'm on a roll.

The Chaser

Prostitute Reviews

With Seth Gordon

◆ Sonia, 24
◆ The Oral Majority, Sydney

Brent ◆
Private Address, Boulder, WA ◆

One of the worst kept secrets in the sex industry is that, many years ago, I used to manage a small brothel on the outskirts of Brisbane.

It was unnotable in almost every respect, except for a brief period when it employed a girl who was arguably the most sought-after 'framer' in the whole of Queensland. A 'framer' was the colloquial term given to girls who specialised in paraplegic customers; so-called because their chief function during intercourse was to act as an effective support frame for their disabled client.

Which brings me to Sonia, a well-oiled framer if ever there was one. Sonia works in the renowned Campbelltown salon, Oral Majority, servicing almost exclusively a handicapped clientele.

The story goes that Sonia was born with a minor club foot herself, and now feels a duty to help those similarly impaired, whose sexual frustration and insecurity she understands all too well.

Ringing up to make my appointment, I was asked what my particular disability was. I politely explained I had none and, after a series of terse negotiations with the management, Sonia was eventually freed to devote 40 minutes to my (relatively) able body.

Her affinity for cripples shows in the rigidity of her touch. Here is a woman expertly trained in a strong grasp, and it wasn't until the climax of our session that she finally allowed herself to loosen up and adapt to the foreign fluidity of my thrust.

In many ways, it's inappropriate for me to review a framer out of her natural context. But from what I glimpsed during our generous tumble, I can assure every chair-prowler out there that Sonia has what it takes. My only quibble is the lack of wheelchair access to her room.

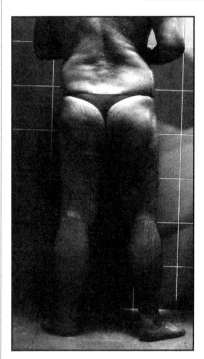

Nobody needs me to tell them that Kalgoorlie is synonymous with prostitution. The tin sheds of Hay Street are virtually a second home for local mining residents and tourists alike. To me Hay Street has always represented the brothel as theme park: a kind of Disney debauchery. One could never be confident of anything too wild taking place in such a colourful cluster of whorehouses. More than anything else, the strip lacks variety.

A fellow critic once challenged me to find a single male hooker in Kalgoorlie. It was a good point: where can a homosexual punter go for a piece of local trade? The answer, I discovered after exhaustive detective work, is to drive roughly 20 km to the next town of Boulder, where in a nondescript residential street stands a green weatherboard shack: a little hideaway salon that's one of Kalgoorlie's best kept secrets.

The shack belongs to Brent (real name), who is just about as far removed from your typical miner as you can get. Pale, effeminate and shy, this twenty something escort sparkles like a spring oasis in an otherwise barren desert of macho aggression and misogyny.

It's early days for Brent's business, as can be evidenced in his nervous, jittery small talk and the various pins which I found still fixed to his new collared shirt. (Some fashion advice Brent: get rid of the corduroy slacks and Van Heusen chemise, and buy yourself something smart from Marcs.)

But it's out of his clothes where Brent comes into his own, proving himself a veritable workhorse of unimagined proportions. The sex is both tender and thorough, characterised by a refreshing lack of inhibition from one so new to the game. A genuine find that's well worth a detour.

The Chaser

UMP Eye Chart

The all-new doctor's eye chart

Test your eyesight using the Department of Health's brand new standardised eye chart. This elegant looking chart *(note: if it looks elegant, you obviously can't see)* has been designed and approved by Australia's leading ophthalmologists, and from next month will be displayed in every doctor's surgery in the country. To examine your eyesight, simply position the chart ten metres from your body, and read out the letters on the bottom line. If you're ten metres away and still managing to read this introductory blurb, then you're not doing too badly at all. Extreme show-offs are encouraged to take the Department's advanced eye test, which involves driving 12 kilometres away to another suburb, putting on a blindfold, and then reading out the letters in the fine print on the reverse side of the chart.

T
OO
BADT
HATYO
URE BLI
NDIWOULD
FIXITBUTSAD
LYIDONTHAVEANY
MEDICALINSURANCE

The Chaser

Tyson agrees to fight in Aussie playground in return for million dollar payout

MARYLAND, Tuesday: Former world heavyweight champion Mike Tyson has announced that his next fight will be held in an Australian schoolyard so that he can secure a massive payout. 'We've heard they pay big money for fights in your Aussie playgrounds,' said promoter Don King.

'Mike will go where the cash is. We were negotiating with a casino in Atlantic City,' King said, 'but they just couldn't match the money the NSW Supreme Court has been handing out.'

King acknowledged that there may be problems organising the Tyson schoolyard fight. 'We have to get him enrolled in a high school for a start. If it was a primary school, Mike might be able to cope, but Year 7 will be a bit of a stretch. Mind you, getting into an Australian high school will be easier than getting him a boxing licence in the US, so we're going with it.'

The Tyson announcement has caused a sensation in boxing and education circles. Former school fighter David Griffin, who was recently awarded $1 million in damages after losing a pre-arranged fight at school, said he is considering coming out of retirement to take on Tyson. 'I'm very confident that I could lose against Tyson', Griffin told reporters. 'I got a million for being knocked out by a bloke in my own year. With the sort of damage Tyson would do me, I reckon I'll get billions'.

The Department of Education, which the Supreme Court found had failed to recognise the potential for violence in schools, yesterday said that it 'did not see any difficulty' with the plan for Tyson to fight in one of its yards. 'We host pre-arranged fights all the time,' said a spokesperson for the Department. 'Usually everyone in the whole school knows about it except the teachers, so we're just glad we know about this fight in advance. Now at least we'll get to watch.'

The spokesperson said the Department would not be taking any special precautions for the Tyson fight, 'As long as he stops when the bell rings, he can basically do what he wants. We don't frown on biting as much as some of the professional boxing associations. In fact it's quite common, though more so in the primary schools.'

Tyson and Don King in the NSW playground that has replaced Las Vegas as the world centre of big-money fighting

The Chaser

Magic eye

Jackson Pollock's masterpiece, *Blue Poles*, makes a lot more sense when you realise it's actually just a Magic Eye game. Hold the image a few centimetres away from your face and blur your eyes until a three-dimensional image of a gullible art critic appears.

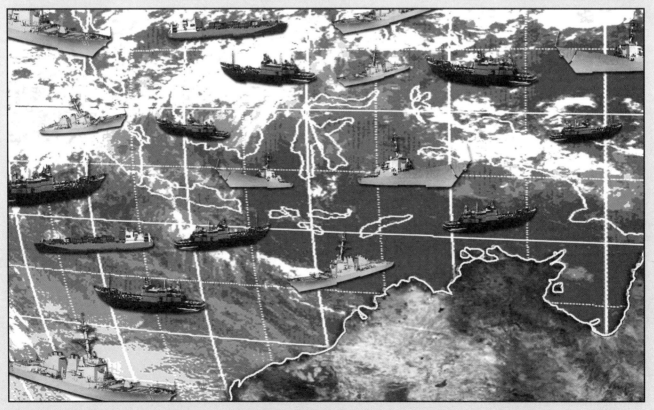

This one's only for government ministers and talkback hosts. Hold the picture close up to your face, then blur your eyes so you start to think you can see children being thrown overboard. One minute they're not there. Next minute they are. It's magic!

The Chaser

24th May 2002

'Episode III' filming in crisis as Ruddock cracks down on illegal aliens

CANBERRA, Tuesday: Immigration Minister Phillip Ruddock has placed the production of *Star Wars Episode III* in jeopardy after deporting 95% of the cast. The movie, which was to be filmed in Australia, was denounced by Ruddock as 'a haven for illegal aliens.' Ruddock declared that almost all of the aliens involved in the production had failed to satisfy the requirements to enter the country, citing immigrants from the planet Kamino as 'particularly slapdash'. 'Australia must retain control over who it lets within its borders. And it's crucial that the Government sends a strong message to people traffickers like George Lucas by sending these illegals on the first starship back to where they came from,' Ruddock told reporters.

Ruddock announced the crackdown after discovering that some of the asylum-seekers had ties to the

Ruddock deports illegal immigrant Jabba the Hutt back to Tatooine

Dark Side of The Force. However, he has expressed misgivings about them for some time. 'Their attempts to assimilate have been atrocious. That Yoda character struggles to speak English even after three years in the country, and I'm particularly

disappointed by the manner in which the clones have brought their war to our shores.' When pressed further, Ruddock retorted, 'Hey, I don't see them taking refugees at all on Planet Naboo.' Ruddock conceded that some of the asylum-

seekers may have fled the tyrannical reign of Count Dooku and so would have legitimate claims. But he maintained this was no excuse to avoid the appropriate channels, declaring them 'simply queue-jumpers.'

The Chaser

US passes free trade subsidy legislation

Bush launches the generous subsidies

WASHINGTON, Tuesday: Responding to the international outrage which followed their recent steel and farm subsidies, the United States has agreed to return to the free trade fold. Speaking at the World Trade Organisation headquarters President Bush agreed to make free trade the number one priority of his administration. 'Today I am promising that every American company engaging in and promoting free trade will receive a whopping subsidy from the government,' Bush said. The change in policy will see the US making its greatest commitment to free trade ever.

'For every dollar in farm subsidies our farmers turn down, we will give them two dollars in free trade subsidies,' said US Democratic leader Joe Lieberman who sponsored the bill before the Senate. 'Now no one can question our commitment to free trade.' Critics of the bill claim it is simply a reflection of the fact that politicians from both sides of politics are captive to free trade lobbyists. The US has historically led nations pushing free trade, particularly as third world markets have been opened up to first world companies. Their ideological fervour has, however, failed to translate into cutting first world subsidies so that the third world can actually trade with it.

Celebrity advice

With special guest
Kathy Lette

Q: I think my friend may have an eating disorder. If we go out to dinner she will only ever order salad and she always disappears to the bathroom soon after she's eaten. I don't know whether I should say something or whether that will only make the situation worse. Help!

A: **Sado Mastication – the real meaning of S and M. Too often in our society we women are JBTB (judged by their bums) and not by their brains – and we suffer facial, rather than racial, prejudice. You've got to talk to your friend and talk to her fast. Why not casually bring it up in conversation that you think she might be 'bringing it up' herself (her dinner that is!). Or just BIO (blurt it out) as a joke. After all, many a true word is spoken ingest. Encourage her to exceed her feed limit.**

Q: I'm 24 and I'm looking for Mr Right but I'm not having any luck. Should I keep trying or just give up?

A: **Don't worry about a Mr Right at your age, you should be looking for a Mr Wrong – they're much more fun! What you need is someone with a pert bum who gives the best cunnilingus this side of a detachable shower nozzle. A so-called Mr Right will soon become the ingrown pube in your bikini wax – he will expect you to iron his shirts and do his EL (emotional laundry) and will then leave you as soon as you're past your amuse-by date.**

Q: I have recently inherited $75000 from a distant relative. Should I invest in real estate or shares?

A: **The share market may go down faster than the English cricket team, real estate is the kind of investment that goes through the Tunnel of Love holding its own hand. Did I mention cunnilingus? Liposuction. Buttocks. Penile augmentation. Episiotomy.**

The Chaser

We Will Remember: The Last Anzac

Government mourns loss of last Anzac: 'That's one less old person we can screw over'

CANBERRA, Wednesday: Treasurer Peter Costello has lamented the death of Alec Campbell, the last surviving Anzac, bemoaning the lost revenue the government could have gained at his expense following the Budget. 'It's an extraordinary loss,' sobbed Costello. 'A $6.20 loss to us per drug prescription, to be precise.' The Treasury Department, which has worked for five years squeezing Australia's elderly and disabled to the point that the government makes profits from them, held a minute's silence to commemorate the 28% hike in pharmaceutical benefits they would have enjoyed had Campbell managed to hang on a few more years. Several Treasury hacks are said to have shed tears when they recalled the copious amounts of asthma medication they were denied exploiting because of his death.

They then honoured a humble memorial for the extra $188 per fortnight they would have reaped when the Budget successfully downgraded Campbell from the ex-servicemen's pension

Costello shows how much money they could have screwed out of Campbell

to the Newstart allowance. 'But it's so much more than simply fiscals,' said Costello. 'It's the long-established Aussie tradition of mean-spirited Treasurers ripping off the less fortunate that has died a little death today. But we will remember.'· Costello presented a short but respectful tribute to Campbell, drawing attention to his long years of service for his country and concluding, 'It's a shame that such a glorious Australian would have given up the fight in his country's hour of need, just when we could have profited most from him.'

French build commemorative airport on last digger's grave

HOBART, Sunday: International tributes have flooded in following the death of Australia's last Gallipoli survivor Alec Campbell at age 103. The French government led the mourning with their offer to build a commemorative airport over the recently deceased digger's grave in Tasmania. Campbell died at a Hobart nursing home in his sleep three weeks ago and was discovered by staff last Thursday. Mr Howard said he was deeply saddened by Mr Campbell's passing. 'It's most upsetting that Australia no longer has any survivors of the original Anzac Day that I can be photographed with,' admitted a sullen Mr Howard.

Tasmanian politicians were unenthusiastic about the proposed runway despite French claims it would be both a 'fitting tribute to a war victim' as well as 'a great way to promote more Franco-Tasmanian tourism'. The French government rejected suggestions that their attempt to start the airport works during the burial ceremony was insensitive. 'We certainly didn't mean any disrespect to Australia's war dead, or at least no more than usual,' the French Ambassador stated at a press conference yesterday. 'We gave the Australian government an undertaking that we would give the family and the country time to go

Air France: forced to abort landing due to Campbell's funeral

through the grieving process, and we did that. Besides, it seemed pointless to let the cement dry and then have to rip it up again.

The Returned Servicemen's League has reacted strongly against the desecration of Mr Campbell's grave, with President Peter Phillips saying the event 'highlighted once again the dangers of becoming a republic or letting more immigrants in.'

Left-winger who 'refuses to eat at McDonald's' has his third Big Mac Meal Deal this month

MELBOURNE, Wednesday: A man who never eats at McDonald's ate his third Big Mac in three weeks last night.

Peter Jones, 34, is ideologically opposed to the fast food chain, which he believes exploits workers.

He has maintained a personal boycott of the restaurants for 12 years, during which time he has eaten 435 Big Macs, 211 Quarter Pounders with Cheese, 380 servings of fries and 670 Cokes.

Mr Jones said the visits were justified because on those occasions he had been 'really pissed' and nothing else was open at 3 a.m. He said that if the people who ran the felafel place down the road bothered to stay open, he would have gone there.

Mr Jones said he thought it was a pity that the workers at McDonald's had to work that late, but maintained that his individual consumption of 'an occasional Big Mac' was hardly going to make McDonald's change its way.

Mr Jones also boycotts Starbucks, including the Swanston St outlet where he sometimes goes before work if he's in a rush.

Jones refuses to eat burger in principle, though not in actual fact

Some generic 'last digger' article we've had on file for years awaiting his death

[CITY, Day]: Australians woke this morning to a country which will forever more be a little sadder after the death of a national hero. Yesterday Australia's last Anzac [INSERT NAME] died [INSERT DEATH] at his home in [INSERT HOME].

[INSERT NAME] was just one of the thousands of Aussies who landed on the beaches of Gallipoli for that fateful campaign which defined us as a nation.

Although [INSERT NAME] has left us his memory will live on forever in our national consciousness.

The Prime Minister [INSERT NAME] reminded all Australians of the debt they owed to the diggers who gave us the freedoms we hold dear today.

Rape-vengeance sprees end after 'Baise-Moi' ban

SYDNEY, Tuesday: Federal Attorney-General Darryl Williams has hailed the banning of French film *Baise-Moi* as a success after no incidents of rape-vengeance killing sprees with lesbian overtones were recorded in the week after the ban was implemented.

'*Baise-Moi* posed a serious threat to our society,' said Williams. 'Although I haven't seen it yet.'

His stance has received unexpected support from pervert quarters. 'We are relieved that *Baise-Moi* has been taken off the screens,' said one pervert. 'It was terrible having to go to those trendy, expensive arthouse cinemas and hang around with those pretentious arty types. Thankfully now people like me can return to getting hard core porn without having to pretend that we're interested in the artistic point.'

Others are grateful for the ban for different reasons. 'I guess I've always had a tendency towards violent sex crime,' said Jack Watson, 37, of Fitzroy, 'I reckon seeing a French arthouse film could have tipped me over the edge. I'm so relieved it's been banned. Thanks to the ban, I've decided against any criminal activity and I think I should be able to keep my sadistic sexual urges under control from now on.'

JUNKY PASTIMES

Andrew Weldon

Shallow graves now 'all the rage' in Melbourne society circles

Mary Wilkins of Toorak: fashionable to her grave

MELBOURNE, Wednesday: Melbourne's most exclusive suburbs have been swept up in a new craze following the death of prominent socialites Paul and Margaret King. Several prominent socialites from Toorak and Brighton have been found burying themselves in shallow graves all around the city.

'I used to think graves were a bit grubby,' said Dimity Kent of Toorak. 'But if Margaret is doing it, then it must be in vogue.'

The children of Melbourne socialites have obliged by asphyxiating their parents, following the trend allegedly set by the Kings' son and stepson, Matthew Wales. 'I normally resent helping my parents do things they consider fashionable, like hosting jazz evenings and helping charitable causes,' said one murderer, Tim Brown of South Yarra. 'But when they asked me to kill them and collect my inheritance early, I thought "hey, this could be pretty cool for me, too."'

Channel Ten's gossip correspondent, Angela Bishop, argues that this is just a passing fad. 'Personally I'd be surprised if people trek off to Gippsland to do this again,' noted Bishop. 'Especially when they find out how devilishly hard it is to get bloodstains out of a Louis Vuitton handbag.'

The Chaser

TIRED of CRAMPS, DIZZINESS, and BOTULISM after eating a slice of Super Supreme?
Then YOUR WORRIES are SOLVED!
Let this *Chaser* How-To Guide™ take you from QUEASY to EASY...as we show you...

AMERICA'S FAVOURITE pizza experience got you CONFUSED?

How to eat a Pizza Hut™ pizza without inordinate suffering

THE FIRST OBSTACLE to overcome in learning to enjoy Pizza Hut pizzas is that you must ALTER your PERCEPTION.

It is vital that you overcome your body's natural aversion to food that is – at first glance anyway! – completely and irredeemably inedible.

Let us begin, young Pizza Padawan.

FIRST, you must obtain a lovely, tepid slab of pizza from your nearest Pizza Hut. Note how the base is not made of boring old DOUGH, but moist, yummy BATTER.

PIZZA TIP #1

Let's face it!

If you're going to digest this pizza, you will need to actually reduce its oil content to something less than what might have seemed reasonable to the emperor Caligula.

This can be achieved by squishing your pizza through an old-fashioned CLOTHES MANGLE.

Mind you don't slip! Your laundry floor will be awash with vegetable oil.

PIZZA TIP #2

Toppings Treasure Hunt!

Have fun with your pizza by going on a TOPPINGS TREASURE HUNT! Join your friends or family in a PIZZA EMU PARADE, where each person minutely scans the surface of the pizza in an attempt to find a bit of topping.

If someone does unearth a little rubber stopper of a bit of meat or a fleck of dark green representing capsicum, they should loudly sing 'Pizza Hut!' to the tune of the jingle.

PIZZA TIP #3

Let's face it!

Be prepared for your rude functions! Fill your dining room with towels, buckets, high-pressure hoses, and oxygen masks.

It is also essential when eating Pizza Hut to have on hand not merely one fully qualified doctor, but a complete squad of elite medical specialists from every field of endeavour, each one trained in emergency and wartime medical procedures.

PIZZA TIP #4

Tone those guts!

You must start a rigorous training program at least six weeks prior to your pizza meal.

You have to allow your stomach and bowels to become hardened and de-sensitised to the brutality of that Hot & Spicy! (Or, the Everest for Pizza Hut attempters, the BBQ Meat Lovers.)

Begin with a few relatively harmless snacks per day – the odd bit of someone's takeaway left lying on the footpath in the sun, or urinal cakes from a public lavatory.

After a fortnight, start on more noxious meals. Sift through the garbage skip out the back of melanoma clinics or veterinarian surgeries. Chug down a can or two of rancid tuna, or run your tongue along the floor of a bus from one end to the other.

A week before the actual pizza, you should no longer be eating safe, regular food. Feast as often as possible on tins of paint, terrifying shards of glass, and exhumed corpses.

Only then will you be ready for a $14.95 Meal for Two!

★ NOW LET'S EAT

While biting into the nauseous body of the Pizza That Should Not Be, it helps if you close your eyes and imagine you're eating something many times nicer, such as a live, struggling funnel web spider.

After choking down a mouthful or two, be ready with those buckets and related equipment, as hurricanes of sour flatulence burble forth from your now useless bottom, and whips of acidic chunder shoot with devastating celerity from your destroyed oesophagus.

Halfway through the Hawaiian Thin & Crispy, or whichever of Pizza Hut's chamber of horrors you've decided upon, don't be surprised to find your team of doctors giving you massive blood transfusions, and trying to restart your lungs.

If you remain alive and conscious until the very last of your pizza has been eaten, WELL DONE! You may apply for a Victoria Cross.

If not, you may find the following funeral specialists both caring and efficient:
• Woronora General Cemetery Crematorium
• Olsens Funerals
• Ann Wilson Funerals
• Simplicity Funerals

LEGAL DISCLAIMER:
Andrew Hansen and everyone at The Chaser really like Pizza Hut, and thoroughly recommend all its menu items.TM

chase up ◆ HELP US BAN THE BIBLE! ◆

The banning of *Baise-Moi* inspired *The Chaser* to campaign for more censorship in Australia.
We are concerned that children, and even adults, are reading stories of incestuous rape and violent vengeance.
Help us by petitioning the Office of Film and Literature Classification to ban The Bible.
Remember, the concerns of a small scaremongering minority justify the use of censorship.

Classification Review Board
Office of Film and Literature Classification
Locked Bag 3 Haymarket NSW 1240

Dear Director,

We would like to congratulate you for your banning of the French rape vengeance film Baise-Moi. We would now like you to ban The Bible which also features substantial examples of rape and vengeance as well as frequent examples of incest.

We understand that you have previously accepted the distribution of The Bible, however, we are aware that you will change your decisions at the petition of a vocal unrepresentative minority.

We also note that The Bible is often forced upon children. Clearly children forced to read The Bible are not in need of the same levels of protection as adults who chose to attend arthouse movie theatres but they may still be impressionable enough to be protected.

Here is merely a selection of the many breaches of your Classification Guidelines:

* **[Rape-vengeance-promotion of violence]** Dinah is raped by Shechem. In an excessive act of vengeance her brothers Simeon and Levi then 'slew all the males' in Shechem's city. Genesis, Chapter 34, verses 1-29

* **[Rape-incest-vengeance]** Amnon rapes his sister Tamar and is then killed by his brother Absalom. Samuel 2, Chapter 13

* **[Rape-incest with father]** Lot is taken to the mountain by his daughters who get him drunk and then sleep with him so that they can 'preserve his seed'. Genesis, Chapter 19, Verses 30-38.

We keenly await your response,

Craig Reucassel

Craig Reucassel
Co-Editor
The Chaser

www.chaser.com.au
Phone: (02) 9380 5051 Fax: (02) 9356 8591

The Chaser

England's World Cup Disaster: Star hooligan breaks foot

CHELSEA, Tuesday: The English World Cup 2002 campaign is in tatters after star hooligan Gerard Wilson of Chelsea broke his foot.

The loss comes at a crucial period for English soccer hooliganism, which faces huge challenges from Germany and is suffering after bans prevented them from training in Europe this season.

The coach of the English hooligans, William Kendall, is frustrated by the disaster.

'Earlier in the year we were primed for Japan and Korea when we got the opportunity to practise on some Asians during the Bradfield race riots,' said Kendall. 'But injuries and arrests are really cutting into our preparation now.'

Wilson's injury is a double blow for the team as he is both the captain and the star striker.

'Wilson is an amazing striker,' said fellow representative hooligan Kevin Jackson of West Ham. 'He can strike with both feet and his head. He's also pretty handy with a baseball bat.'

The selection of the national team was greatly hindered by the government who banned 1,007 of England's best hooligans from travelling overseas.

'We are really taking a B-grade team but luckily there is a lot of depth in England,' said Kendall. 'These guys don't have the natural talent but with enough lager under their belt I still think we can win.'

England's main rival at this year's World Cup will be Germany, who have managed to incorporate the broader political statement of a return to Nazism into their soccer hooliganism.

A nation with a proud tradition of World Cup soccer hooliganism anxiously awaits Wilson's return

The Chaser

Cronje dead after crash: Denies plane was fixed

CAPE TOWN, Saturday: Disgraced former South African cricket captain Hansie Cronje was killed today when flying through a storm in a plane that he maintains 'was not fixed'.

'I swear the outcome of that tour wasn't meddled with,' Cronje has insisted repeatedly from beyond the grave. 'When I found out the plane's performance was unpredictable I was tempted briefly to tamper with it but I wasn't going to make that mistake again.'

Nevertheless authorities' suspicions were aroused after the plane, which had previously recorded sixty consecutive successful outings, went down. Even more suspect, the crash is said to have offered Cronje, who gambled on the flight, a good spread.

Indian flight controllers have already released secret tapes of private calls made to Cronje by a mystery man, thought to be the owner of the cargo plane, imploring him to have it fixed. It has been said that sums of money in the order of $US1000, almost enough for the servicing of a plane, were offered to Cronje for the job.

Several shady figures from the world of aeronautical mechanics have also come forward, admitting to dealings with Cronje in which they discussed the underperformance of planes.

But Cronje's crash has still come as a great shock to the South African cricket fraternity. South African Chief Executive Ali Bacher told reporters, 'For someone who made a career out of giving weather reports, he really got this one wrong.'

Nevertheless, Bacher remained hopeful he would yet be reunited with Cronje. 'Being such a devout Christian, there's

Cronje: fatal crash after losing phone contact with Indian bookmakers

every chance he may be born again again,' he said.

The news fell heaviest upon Justice Edwin King, the man who oversaw the enquiry that ended Cronje's career. 'I feel a certain degree of responsibility for Hansie's death,' he confessed. 'I only wish I'd made it clear to Hansie that his life ban extended solely to playing cricket.'

'60 Minutes' outbids George Pell for rights to sex abuse story

SYDNEY, Sunday: '60 Minutes' has won a bidding war against Sydney's Catholic Archbishop Dr George Pell over the exclusive rights to a story about sex abuse by a priest. The agent for David Ridsdale confirmed that the abuse victim had been negotiating with Dr Pell on a price for him not to speak about his molestation, but that Ridsdale had received a better offer from '60 Minutes' to tell the story.

While the public has reacted negatively to the Church's attempt to buy Ridsdale's silence, his agent has a different perspective. 'We weren't really appalled at the Church offering money for the story, it was just the amount on offer that got us offside.'

'It really came down to a choice between cheque-book journalism and cheque-book confidentiality,' the agent acknowledged.

'60 Minutes' producers said they were happy to secure the Ridsdale story. 'We usually pay the BBC for Richard Carleton's stories, so this was a nice change,' said one executive. The executive said it was difficult to compete with the Catholic Church. 'They'd made David a pretty attractive kiss and no-tell arrangement. But then Pell offered to throw in an indulgence as well, and that kind of freaked him out.'

Ridsdale's decision to speak to '60 Minutes' has produced severely negative publicity for the Catholic Church.

It is understood that Archbishop Pell was considering engaging the PR firm used by Governor-General and former Anglican Archbishop of Brisbane Peter Hollingworth to help him inflame the situation by making damaging and insensitive comments.

But Pell has decided against using the firm and will instead rely on his natural capacity to handle the situation poorly.

The suicide builders have run demolitions near the Wailing Wall for years

Palestine retaliates against new Israeli wall with suicide builders

WEST BANK, Thursday: Palestinian resistance groups yesterday responded to Israel's plan to build a Berlin Wall-esque defensive barrier around the West Bank by announcing the recruitment of a squad of particularly shoddy construction workers they dubbed 'suicide builders'.

'Israel must realise that until they respond to our demands we will bring the war to them,' said builder Abdul Yafettah. 'If they wish to cowardly attack us with their military might then we will bomb them. And if they wish to cowardly attack us with their proficient workmanship then we will build right back at them until they understand.'

Unfortunately, without the enormous resources the Israelis can command for their barrier, solitary Palestinians have had to erect entire razor wire fences without implements, ensuring their certain death.

Regardless of the danger, several lone workers have already attacked Tel Aviv with a wave of construction. Birdbaths, cabinets and pagodas have all been erected in busy urban centres, and even a wedding reception has been disturbed by the creation of a rudimentary sculpture of Michael Schumacher.

Nervous West Bank residents are prisoners in their own homes, fearing retribution from the Israelis. 'I don't know what form it will take, but it will be big,' a Palestinian woman told reporters. 'It could be an airport, a skyscraper or even a rail network. They built whole settlements even before the fighting.'

US President George W. Bush is said to be awaiting 'further developments'.

Archbishop Pell comforts another victim of clerical sexual abuse

New Zealand rebadged 'The All-New Zealand'

Clark launches her country's exciting new brand name

WELLINGTON, Thursday: New Zealand Prime Minister Helen Clark has announced that her country will be renamed 'The All-New Zealand' in an attempt to improve its appeal to tourists. 'Hundreds of years ago, the prospect of visiting a new version of Zealand was enticing, but the name has stayed the same for so long, the message of newness was just getting lost,' Clark said. 'The new name successfully communicates that what we are offering is an exciting new twist on the much-loved Zealand brand.'

Clark says she got the idea for the name from a commercial radio station in Perth when she was recently in Australia. 'When I tuned into the All-New 92.9, I thought to myself 'I know what else is all-new – and it's even bigger, being a whole country and all,' she said. 'Plus, like their music, NZ was the best in the 70s, 80s, 90s – and now. Well, at least at rugby.'

The name change process has been controversial. Following on from the nation's appearance in the *Lord of the Rings* trilogy, there was a strong push for it to be renamed 'Ye Olde Zealande'. There was also strong support from minimalist designers for 'newzealand', while the nation's burgeoning Internet industry wanted it renamed simply '.nz'.

But Clarke thinks that the new name will have popular appeal. 'Stressing the benefits of our wonderful geography – as well as appealing to older customers – will take place in our TV ads, which will focus on the benefits of our "hills and memories" format,' she said.

The renaming has started an international trend of rethinking placenames. To cast a positive light on the extensive rebuilding that is taking place after September 11, New York will rename itself 'Even Newer York.' Also, in an attempt to disassociate itself from a place that most consumers thought was boring, the Australian state of New South Wales will be renamed 'Not At All Like South Wales.'

Refined teen plays 'air bassoon' in front of bedroom mirror

ADELAIDE, Sunday: A cultivated male teenager was last night observed inside his bedroom, playing 'air bassoon' in front of a full-length mirror.

The 17-year-old student was rapturously miming syncopated bassoon fingering along with a Brahms concerto which was playing loudly on his CD player.

The cultured teen said he liked to fantasise in front of the mirror, pretending he was playing first bassoon in one of Europe's major concert halls. He said he thought blowing into an imaginary woodwind reed, in addition to its escapism value, was a wonderful way to release pent-up teenage angst.

'Often when I go to live recitals, I like to stand right up the front with the other teenagers so I can air bassoon with them in the mosh pit,' he said.

The boy's parents said that in previous years they've also caught him in his bedroom playing air oboe, air timpani and air French horn.

The air bassoonist 'going off' during the concerto's lively presto movement

First ever Persian rug sold at full price

CARLTON, Saturday: The designer floor covering world is in shock this week after a hand-made silk Persian rug was purchased for full price. The startling sale occurred at the Carlton branch of the Rug Hut carpet chain. An industry commission has been established to investigate why the carpet was 'sold' instead of being liquidated.

'I had tried reducing the hand-made traditional Persian rug to half price, going out of business and stocking our factory warehouses to the point where we could hold no more high quality carpets, but it just wouldn't sell,' said franchise owner, Philip Hamaad. 'Finally I just decided to try and "sell" the carpet, and somebody fell for it.'

The rug industry has not seen such turmoil since 1999 when Omar Kahn's Persian King rug store closed down during a closing down sale.

Hamaad: a remarkable rug innovator

Unions concerned public may believe Crean runs the ALP

GOLD COAST, Wednesday: ALP conference delegates representing the trade union movement have expressed reservations about Labor's proposed abolition of the traditional 60 – 40 rule, feeling it may mislead the public into believing Simon Crean has influence in the Labor Party.

The rule, which ensures the Union movement has 60% input into Labor Party decisions, is seen as vital to a party desperately trying to distance itself from suggestions it is simply a voicebox for Mr Crean.

'We have a crucial election coming up in the year 2005,' said ACTU President Sharan Burrow, 'And the last thing we need is to fall victim to community prejudice against Crean. Costello and Abbott are already equating him with the Labor Party to score political points.'

While Burrow acknowledged the good work done by Simon Crean over the years, she felt that the constant negative images of Crean that voters had been subjected to had finally taken their toll. 'The introduction of new laws meaning it's no longer compulsory to support Crean didn't help either,' she lamented.

However, Crean defended

Crean: an embarrassing link the ALP is trying to live down

himself, noting, 'The Labor Party identifies itself with the battler struggling against the odds, and if ever there was a battler struggling just to keep his head above the water, I would have thought that would be me.'

The Opposition Leader also rejected suggestions the issue was dividing the Labor Party, 'I've got a terrific track record at promoting party unity,' said Crean. 'When I rose to power the Labor Party was riven with factions. But today the entire party is united against me.'

Miss Universe competition biased, claims Martian beauty

MARS, Wednesday: Martian beauty queen Xzyryryyl Sclblcb, has lashed out angrily at what she described as the deep and persistent prejudice that mars the Miss Universe Competition.

Speaking at an intergalactic press conference, Miss Sclblcb criticised the anthropocentric focus of the popular beauty pageant.

'All of the contestants have consistently been human. The judges are human. And quite frankly, I think it's outrageously arrogant to claim that a few Earthling women from different geopolitical areas of that pissy planet represent the entire Universe.'

Since the outburst, glamour queens from several other planets have also spoken out in support of her sentiments. Miss Venus, Aaaaeioioi Blblbblblb, complained that the beauty standards were too heavily based on human aesthetics.

'The judges make their decision based on a one-headed, two-eyed, two-armed, two-legged being with pink or brown skin. You're not going to find a triple-breasted, four-legged Venusian winning any prizes in the bikini competition. And the girls from Neptune – well, they can just forget it'.

Organisers of the Miss Universe competition have dismissed the criticisms as 'ridiculous', stating that the competition is open to all intergalactic beauties who wish to enter. However, speaking candidly to reporters, pageant organiser Mrs Dallas Parcheut stated that the entries were in fact restricted to Earthlings to 'give the Americans a better chance at winning'.

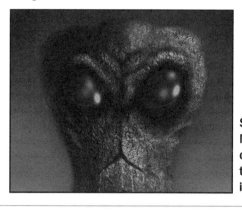

Sclblcb says the Miss Universe competition is less than genuinely interplanetary

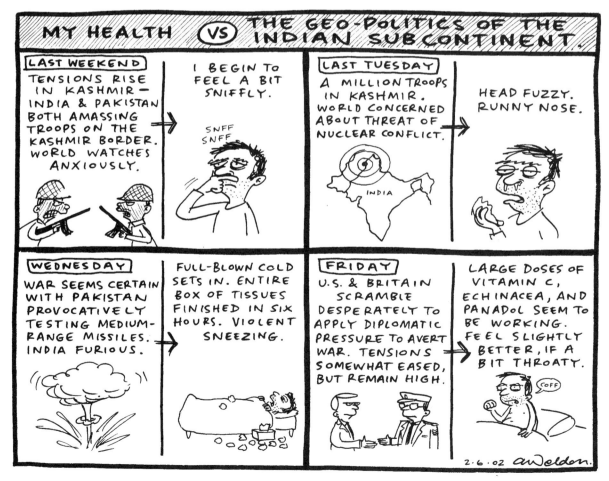

Ever dream about retiring to a Caribbean island?

Discover Dreams

The world's most secluded residential development, Camp X-Ray, is pleased to announce the release of 110 privately appointed apartments for you to own and enjoy. Don't miss this extraordinary opportunity to invest in a simpler, more secure lifestyle.

Discover Solitude

No more noise. No more bustle. No more hassles. At Camp X-Ray you'll feel completely removed from the rest of the world. Tranquility has a new name – and it's called Camp X-Ray.

Discover Living

Every apartment at Camp X-Ray boasts the very latest in sleek minimalist design. Each individual room is also fitted with world-class security features, making Camp X-Ray one of the most secure places to live in the whole world.

Discover Location

Camp X-Ray enjoys a stunning position in Guantanamo Bay, overlooking the world-renowned Caribbean Sea. Feel the turquoise water lap at your feet, as you're briskly herded off a US Navy transport ship and into your new home.

Discover Camp X-Ray

What's in a name? The "X" is for eXquisite. The "Ray" is for the constant sun beams that will flood into your new home. The "Camp" is for the US drill sergeant who keeps coming into your room in the middle of the night.

Camp X-Ray Features

- First-class security
- Unhurried lifestyle
- On-site barber

CUBA

Guantanamo Bay Holiday Resort

JAMAICA

Caribbean Sea

Discover Camp X-Ray for yourself. Once there, you'll never leave.

The Chaser

Tony Abbott slams quadriplegic job snob

WERRINGTON, Thursday: Workplace Relations Minister Mr Tony Abbott has exposed the existence of yet another job snob in Sydney's western suburbs. Nathan Masters, a quadriplegic former carpenter, told the Centrelink office last month that he is unwilling to just take any old job that comes along.

According to Abbott, Masters failed to attend not one, not two, but three job interviews organised for him by the local Job Network. 'Apparently, working as a brickie, a kitchen hand or pizza deliverer is not good enough for Masters,' Mr Abbott told Parliament yesterday.

Masters responded to the allegations, but failed to deny Abbott's allegations. 'I'd love to participate in the workforce and be independent, with my own money coming in,' he slurred in his small suburban flat which he shares with a full-time carer.

According to Abbott, these excuses are not good enough. 'Sure, he'd like to work. But only on his terms,' said an unrepentant Abbott. 'Why? Masters is a job snob. He baulks at manual labour and has unrealistic expectations about life in the working world.

'And it's a growing problem', according to Abbott. 'The problem with people like Nathan is they expect they should just waltz into a job where they use their brain rather than their brawn. But life isn't like that,' says Abbott. 'In fact, some manual work might do Nathan some good. All he seems to do is lie around all day.'

His Centrelink caseworker, Sue O'Calligan, agrees. 'When he attends our monthly

Abbott: quadriplegics should stand up and be counted

meeting, all I get out of him is a couple of grunts and some eye rolling,' she says. 'Sometimes it seems like he would need a helping hand just to go to the bathroom.'

Executive presents PowerPoint eulogy at mother's funeral

SYDNEY, Tuesday: A corporate affairs manager from a leading Sydney company yesterday delivered a moving presentation at his mother's funeral, utilising the many features of Microsoft's PowerPoint software.

Before a packed congregation of relatives and friends, the senior executive paid tribute to his mother through a series of bullet points, graphic charts and bold-font mission statements.

He spoke lovingly of his mother's varied passions and interests, represented clearly by an animated pie graph. The eulogy also included estimated projections showing where his mother would be positioned in 10 years' time, had she not been struck dead by lymphatic cancer.

In recognition of her momentous life, the son agreed to divide his oration into three different seminar sessions, titled Early Forecasts, Key Achievements and Growth Outlook.

Tea and coffee were served in between each eulogy session, allowing delegate mourners the chance to meet and chat, or just stretch their legs.

The bereaved executive son said afterwards he thought the

'On message': mourners were impressed by the eulogy's sensitive use of concise summary data in an easy-to-absorb format

presentation was well received, but that he was sorry the tender story of how his mother and father met had to be dropped from the eulogy, when his laptop froze, leaving a large warning dialogue box projected onto the screen above the coffin.

PAKISTAN AVOIDS WAR, SETTLES FOR NUCLEAR TESTS ON INDIA

ISLAMABAD, Monday: Pakistan has today launched a program designed to test India's ability to survive an unprovoked, devastating nuclear barrage. Following three recent missile tests, the new program is expected to test as many as all of the nuclear warheads currently at Pakistan's disposal.

But Pakistani President Pervez Musharraf has assured the international community that the tests are 'routine and nothing to do with our current tensions with India.'

'Pakistan does not seek war with India. We simply wish to establish how effective our nuclear weapons would be if indeed a war did break out,' Musharraf announced. 'We are especially interested in their effect on the 1 million Indian troops amassed on our border, India's entire nuclear arsenal and their Foreign Minister.'

Rejecting assertions that his acts were highly aggressive, Musharraf rather labelled them 'inquisitive'.

The latest rounds follow a full program of testing the use of militant insurgent attacks on a variety of unprepared Indian targets, including Kashmiri border police and the Delhi Parliament. However, Musharraf described the results of that series as 'unsatisfactory'.

Repeating his commitment to pulling the subcontinent back from the brink of war, Musharraf foreshadowed a number of peace initiatives which he sought to canvass with his Indian counterpart, including unconditional Indian surrender and/or annihilation at the hands of a nuclear hailstorm.

Musharraf appealed to Indian Prime Minister Atal Vajpayee to meet for talks 'anywhere, anytime' although he cautioned against holding them in India where Pakistan is also currently conducting routine radioactive fallout testing.

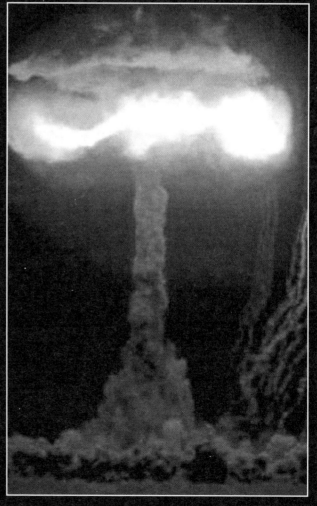

Pakistan carefully tests how many Indian citizens one of its largest nuclear weapons can annihilate

NANCY CRICK'S

HOW TO HOST A EUTHANASIA

TAKES MONTHS TO PREPARE!

BUT IT'S EASY TO PLAY!

COMING SOON:
Bruce Burrell's
How to Host a
Kerry Whelan
Murder

HOW TO HOST A EUTHANASIA

**SGT PETER MCINTOSH
QUEENSLAND POLICE**

Thanks to intense lobbying from Pro-Life campaigners, you've got to attend the scene. You're the most junior officer in your station and you've drawn the short straw. Hang around outside the Crick house and try to work out what the hell you're doing there.

HOW TO HOST A EUTHANASIA

**SALLY-ANNE HISLOP
MEDIA**

Ambitious young reporter looking to make a big impression. Hang outside the Crick house preparing sympathetic looks and catchy death puns to litter your report with. Pace around on your mobile, trying to convince your producer to cross to you for an update. Bring a book because nobody will talk to you all evening.

HOW TO HOST A EUTHANASIA

**TOM HUGHES
BARRISTER**

Spend the pre-death hours boring people about how important you are. While the body's still warm, deliver a stinging eulogy that criticises various people in the room.

HOW TO HOST A EUTHANASIA

**KYM WILSON
ACTOR**

A must for any high profile death. Role does not require much acting talent, and you can quietly leave the scene before the authorities arrive.

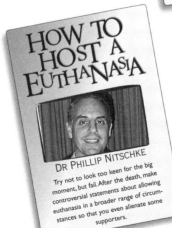

HOW TO HOST A EUTHANASIA

DR PHILLIP NITSCHKE

Try not to look too keen for the big moment, but fail. After the death, make controversial statements about allowing euthanasia in a broader range of circumstances so that you even alienate some supporters.

At last, the game you've been campaigning for years to get...
Nancy Crick's How to Host a Euthanasia game

There are roles for everyone to play!

HOW TO HOST A EUTHANASIA

**NANCY CRICK
HOSTESS, VICTIM**

A once in a lifetime opportunity to showcase your acting flair. It's a very demanding role. Prepare by losing half your body weight and experiencing constant physical pain. Prepare a final entry to your web diary.

And if you're really lucky, you might get to play a star

How to Host a Euthanasia comes with instructions for assembling a deadly cocktail, "all by yourself"!

**How to Host a Euthanasia –
you'll be dying to play again.**

Suitable for ages 60+ (younger with selected diseases).

Carr releases world's first poll-driven novel

SYDNEY, Friday: NSW Premier Bob Carr has completed his first book *Thoughtlines*, the first ever poll-driven novel which Carr promised will also be tough on crime.

Carr said he was happy with the book overall, though he was sad he had to drop his favourite chapter after it got a poor response in focus groups. Critics have labelled the new book uncontroversial and unsatisfying but said that it wasn't bad enough to make them buy another book instead.

The book will be in stores on Monday selling for $29.95, although after a reader backlash at the high price, Carr agreed to make it free for those living in the west of Sydney through a complex rebate system.

The book includes several chapters of a yet to be completed novel which Carr says he will finish if they get a good response.

'If people like them, I will go ahead with the book, but if people don't, I will immediately back down and blame those chapters entirely on a junior minister,' said Carr.

Despite the semi-autobiographical nature of some chapters, journalists claimed they failed to find one juicy revelation about Carr's personal life.

'Those revelations about a boy finding the joy of becoming a Civil War buff were kind of interesting though,' said one journalist.

Following the release of Carr's book Liberal leader John Brogden said that he was also going to release a book. His publisher claimed it would be broadly similar to the Carr book although with slight changes to make it seem younger and slightly tougher on crime. Speaking at the launch a jubilant Mr Carr commented that just about the only thing about the book that hadn't been polled was the cover. Mr Carr's face appears on the cover.

Carr checks focus group feedback before correcting proofs

Prostitute Reviews

With Seth Gordon

◆ Wilma, 23
◆ On Golden Pond, Sydney CBD

There's an old adage that says there are two types of people who go to prostitutes: the happily married and the unhappily single. Lately the clientele might be just as neatly sorted into two other distinct types: those who like to be urinated on, and those who don't.

Since its first lofty trickle, the spectacle of the Golden Shower has caused divisions amongst even the most hardened perverts. Disciples of de Sade hail it as the apotheosis of human indignity; a valuable act of submission and punishment which keeps us in our place. Conservative sex scholars, however, regard it as uniquely crude and unhygenic. The girls at On Golden Pond, I suspect, sit somewhere in between.

This boutique industry bordello has been specialising in urine-based fantasies for the last three years. Clients assemble in the salon's plush bar, where the ladies themselves teasingly mingle,

nursing the very drinks which they'll shortly expel. Keeping the fluids up is essential to the job. Perhaps against my better judgment, I order the house speciality: the Midas Downpour. A petite brunette named Wilma is assigned to my side, and escorts me up the narrow spiral staircase to our bed, freshly fitted with plastic wipe-down sheets.

Only a tiny thing, Wilma's pelvic bones barely look as if they could house a bladder big enough for the task. But that's where I'm wrong. As she positions herself into a commanding squat, she discharges a few loose squirts, by way of testing her aim. Once settled on a trajectory, she emits a steady jet of tepid nectar which splashes hard against my face. She holds her line well, describing a slight parobolic arc, whose faint peripheral spray throws up a rainbow in the bedside light. I won't pretend I'm a convert, but this is as good a golden shower as I've had anywhere the world over. And devotees should note that the salon's now offering Brown Typhoons too.

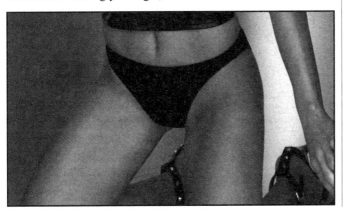

◆ Ronald, 54 ◆
No fixed abode, Darlinghurst, NSW ◆

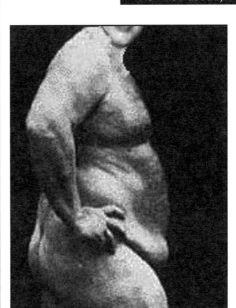

Poor old Ronald. At 54 years of age, he'd have to be the oldest rent boy in the world still working.

A permanent fixture on the Darlinghurst scene, Ronald can be found most days waddling up and down Burton St, eager to sound a scam or a complaint to anyone who will listen. Illness has slowed him down in recent years, but he still likes to turn the occasional trick – more for the company, one suspects, than for the money.

But then it always was about the companionship for Ronald. He's the only trader I know who never minds when a session exceeds the agreed time. He'll happily keep talking long after the meter's expired. In fact, for his

clients, it's usually difficult to get away. I ran into the loveable sod after a recent meal in the district and, motivated in equal parts by charity and nostalgia, agreed to throw him some bills for a crusty once over. It had to be back at my place.

Long gone are the days when Ronald smuggled his customers into the Salvos' infirmary. They used to turn a blind eye, but it would never happen now. Equally unsporting is the staff at St Vincent's Hospital, where Ronald – legend has it – used to whisk his startled clients onto any spare bed he could find. He apparently used to make the clients fabricate a serious injury to guarantee their entry to the ward.

Twenty years on, Ronald forced me to fabricate nothing but my sexual attraction to him, as I set him down on my queen size bed (needn't have changed the sheets that morning in hindsight) and blandly prodded his pale, lumpy flesh. Twelve hours later he was still in my room, babbling on and on. Poor old Ronald.

The Chaser

Train shock: Man slides across seat

The train on which the unprecedented arse-shifting occurred

A WORLD-LEVELLING report has come in of a middle-aged man on a Sydney train who slid his arse 60 centimetres across the seat to allow another passenger to sit down in the aisle position.

The arse-sliding guerilla, Robert Saint, maintains that he is sane.

The consequences of Australia harbouring an arse-shifter of a man like Robert Saint are dire

'It was a morning like any other,' he said. 'I was sitting on a three-person seat in the train, and I was next to the aisle. There was a lady sitting by the window, and between me and her there was a space.

'An arse-sized space, for a third passenger.

'Seeing this fellow standing in the aisle gesturing that he wanted to sit on our seat, I thought damn this all to hell, I'm going to be reckless.

'Rather than making a token diagonal with my legs to "allow" this standing fellow to clamber over me and into the centre of the three seat-spaces, kneecapping me with his boot-heels and clawing bestially at someone in the seat in front's scalp to maintain his balance, which is what would usually happen, I revolutionised the whole procedure by actually shifting myself across into the centre space.

'This had an extraordinary effect. My manoeuvre left the aisle space – which previously had been occupied by none other than myself and my entire body – completely and indubitably free for the man to sit in with ease!'

Saint's foolish method of spontaneous, unauthorised seat allocation was slammed by the NSW Minister for Transport [name withheld].

'It's dangerous, it's recalcitrant or something, and it's unlawful for all I know,' he said.

'All I can say is if you know of any supposed do-gooder sliding across train seats in this manner, leaving room willy-nilly for lazy, predatory standing passengers, you should approach the nearest guard, who you will find no more than seven stops away, and inform them immediately.'

The consequences of Australia harbouring an arse-shifter of a man like Robert Saint are dire, with the United Nations moving to expel us.

Christian church groups are calling for Robert Saint to be condemned to Hell without delay for outrageous behaviour that flies in the face of God, while fundamentalist Muslims have unanimously decided he is the anti-Allah.

The standing passenger, Mr Du Cheng, holds a different opinion, and was choked up during his interview.

'It is unbelievable that a person would make this sacrifice for me,' he said.

'I did nothing to deserve it.

'I was completely ready to scale this man like a flesh Kilimanjaro in order to claim the middle space on the seat.

'And then he pulled this stunt of moving across to let me in.

'I was so amazed and so thankful I could hardly breathe. Instead of sitting in the free aisle spot, I fell to my knees and sobbed with gratitude.

'He didn't even know what station I was planning to get off at. For all he knew, he'd have to surmount my unworthy frame like a human K2 at some later time in order to alight from the train.

'Because buggered if I'd stand up to let him out.'

Meanwhile, CityRail has responded to the event with a public education campaign called 'Train Training!™'

Each Sydney train station will be conducting free workshops for the community where you can learn the best passenger clambering techniques to get you into that centre space as quickly as possible, leaving you more time to relax and enjoy your journey.

Man unsure where to pee in trendy restaurant bathroom

SYDNEY, Friday: A patron at a hip new Sydney restaurant was last night left bewildered inside its bathroom, unable to work out where he was supposed to relieve himself.

The baffled diner said the ultra-minimalist design of the restroom left it virtually featureless, with no obvious area or installation set up for ablutions.

'There was definitely no trough, as you and I would conventionally know it,' the man said. 'Indeed nothing resembling a bowl or receptacle of any kind at all. It was pretty much just four walls and a mirror. For all I know, maybe you were just meant to go on the floor.'

The customer said he opted to hold on until he got home, rather than risk the social faux pas of urinating in the wrong area. 'I mean, I was 80 % sure that the glass wall with the narrow sluice at its base was probably the toilet,' he said. 'But I wasn't going to bank on it. And Christ knows where you stood if you needed to do a number two.'

The man said he noticed that other patrons in the bathroom were equally uncertain about where to go. Many struggled also, he observed, to master the washroom's fashionable hand basin, which discharged water in unsatisfactory amounts at erratically random intervals.

Despite closely examining every ultramodern surface, the man ultimately couldn't work out where he was supposed to urinate

Fire alarm successfully detects actual fire

WEST END, Saturday: A fire alarm detected a real fire last night, a Brisbane man has claimed.

It was the 578th time the alarm had gone off since it was installed in May, but the first time an actual flame had been anywhere near the alarm.

The owner of the alarm, Mr Hugh Linley said he was pleased that he now knew the alarm worked in the presence of smoke because 'up until this point I only knew for certain that it worked not in the presence of smoke.'

Mr Linley said that he had been using the alarm as a 'toast detector' to tell him when his toast was ready. He said the device also was also 'incredibly useful' if he ever needed to wake up at random points during the night, or detect someone smoking next door.

Last night the alarm went off at around 10:30 pm alerting Mr Linley to a fire which had destroyed his house only hours earlier.

Allan Fels says the ACCC will not allow the merger if the rate of *Gilligan's Island* reruns screened is threatened

ACCC condemns Foxtel-Optus merger as 'anti-repetitive'

CANBERRA, Tuesday: The Australian Competition and Consumer Commission has ruled today that the proposed content sharing arrangement between Foxtel and Optus Vision would constitute anti-repetitive conduct.

'This is a clear violation of the Staid Practices Act,' said Commission chairman Professor Allan Fels. 'As a result of this proposal we could see two weather channels reduced to one and four finance channels reduced to two, not to mention the devastating potential effects on the home shopping networks.'

'Make no mistake, this deal means less consumer choice – less choice about which channels to flick past hurriedly and less choice about which channels to watch when stoned.'

The competition watchdog has been monitoring both pay TV networks carefully since their inception for signs of monotonistic behaviour.

But the Commission's hand was forced by the latest deal, offering unprecedentedly low access to Australian television for shithouse programming.

Of particular concern to the ACCC was Foxtel's potential acquisition of Optus' content in the advent of Optus' failure. 'That would mean Foxtel would acquire a virtual monopoly in boutique country music programming,' said Fels. 'Then nothing could stop them.'

Foxtel and Optus have already entered negotiations with the regulator, offering a wide range of options designed to increase the levels of inanity of any joint venture.

Amongst the proposals on the table are tripling the number of hours each consortium spends advertising itself and quadrupling the number of *Gilligan's Island* marathons.

spit *or* swallow?

An advice column for the modern era.

Dear Spit,

Recently I read a book called *Women Who Love Too Much*, and discovered I was one of them. Frightened by my rapture, I murdered my lover in the night and fled. I'm hiding under a rock and am too afraid to emerge. Help me.
Gay Vargas

Dear Gay,
It's awful to realise love can get out of control, but you've done the right thing by exorcising the source of your senility. A life of singledom and coldness will save you from getting hurt, but leave you with little to live for.

Dear Spit,

At a recent party I was so excited talking to a potential doodle holder that I ate a whole packet of salty nuts, plus the wooden bowl they were presented in. The girl thought it was a party trick, but when my face turned red and I fell to the floor with a shameful splat, I lost her respect. Can I reclaim my credibility?
Lacklin Foy

Dear Lacklin,
Forget about your credibility and concentrate on repairing your internal organs which will have been cut and salted badly. Swallowing wood and peanuts in one go can bring on testicular menangitis, which leads to an ejaculation that smells of bar nuts and beer – the ultimate turn off.

Israel unleashes its full wrath on Palestine after its half wrath fails again

Our analysis shows the current half wrath, and the inevitable effect of full wrath

TEL AVIV, Friday: Israeli Prime Minister Ariel Sharon today announced that Israel would unleash its full wrath against Palestine following another spate of suicide bombings. The escalation is seen as a final acceptance of the failure of their previous policies of 'unlea shing half wrath'.

Today's move comes as part of a full scale reassessment of Israel's policy towards Palestine. Amongst other initiatives, President Sharon has now decided that Israel will seek out vengeance rather than waiting for it to find them.

Palestinians expressed shock at the Israeli policy change. 'I must admit that when the Israelis took over the West Bank, flattened Jenin and destroyed our entire infrastructure I felt pretty confident that they had unleashed their full wrath already,' said one Palestinian. 'At the very least it must have been nine tenths worth of wrath.'

Meanwhile sporting coaches in Israel have demanded the government goes in harder against the terrorists. 'Nothing but 110% wrath is enough,' said one coach.

The policy change comes as Israel considers several plans to go back into Palestine.

'We keep taking our military into Palestine for short periods but as soon as we leave the Palestinians get angry and start blowing themselves up,' said Prime Minister Ariel Sharon. 'I think they miss us, so we are considering going back into Palestine full time.'

Israel has reacted more cautiously to a United States backed plan which seeks to copy the Marshall plan used in post World War II Germany. The plan would see Israel help to rebuild Israel and create more employment and economic prosperity as a way of preventing suicide bombings.

Ariel Sharon has at the very least agreed to help increase employment in Palestine.

'Over the coming week we intend to create hundreds of jobs for Palestinians,' said Sharon. 'Palestinians with skills in undertaking and fixing houses hit by mortar shells will particularly benefit from our new employment scheme.'

Jamie Packer defends Jodhi split: 'I was profoundly misled'

BONDI, Thursday: James Packer has released a statement denying responsibility for the failure of his marriage to Jodhi Meares, saying he was 'profoundly misled' about the prospects of his high profile business venture with the former swimsuit model.

'All the initial forecasts were very positive. Jodhi told me that she had an ambitious business plan and I really believed that the partnership could work', Mr Packer said.

Sources say that father Kerry Packer was sceptical about the merits of the venture from the start and made his feelings known to his son.

But Packer Junior defended his proposal, telling his father to 'look at the figure'.

James Packer now says he was deceived about the real state of the marriage. 'I didn't really follow the cashflow in the early days. I had no idea that spending was out of control.'

Packer says he only discovered the truth about his relationship days before the couple split. 'When I found out the actual figures, I was shocked. I considered injecting more money to try and stabilise the arrangement, but by then the model was just no longer viable.'

The separation is the second major failure Mr Packer has had to avoid taking responsibility for in the last 12 months. Sources close to Mr Packer say he is throwing himself into his work after the split, describing his attitude as 'damage control as usual'.

Packer says he has learned a lot from his failures. 'I'm starting to think I shouldn't go into business with Jodees at all,' he admitted.

James Packer looks at the figure

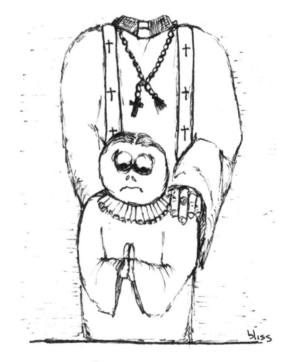

ALTERED BOY

Andrew Bliss

EXTRAORDINARY AUSTRALIANS

From managed funds to reinsurance: one man follows his dream

For many people a job is a job. A necessity of life and a way to earn money – nothing more. But for David Underhill work became much more than that three months ago, when he moved from the soul-destroying drudgery of managed funds, to follow his life's dream – reinsurance.

'At first, I was hesitant about the move. After all, it involved a pay cut from $260,000 to $240,000 and I knew I'd have

to make some lifestyle changes. But that's a small price to pay for a sense of personal fulfilment,' Underhill says.

Since his earliest days, the former financial consultant had longed for a career in re-insurance. 'When I was about seven, I developed an interest in insurance. From there, it was only one small step to reinsurance.'

It was the cut and thrust of

risk management consulting and the dream of leveraging the risk of some of the world's top insurance companies that initially fired Underhill's passion. But it was the day-to-day satisfaction of a job as a reinsurance associate that clinched the deal. 'Drafting contract documentation, calculating and processing financial adjustments, securing periodic banking funding and calculating reinstatement premiums – it's all there,' he enthuses.

After leaving school, Underhill felt he was pushed into a career in managed funds. It was considered the 'safe option', a career where he could enjoy a steady income but not the heady heights and electric excitement of reinsurance. Then, after 13 years working as a managed funds analyst and consultant, Underhill chanced upon a job advertisement in the *Australian Financial Review*. He's never looked back.

'I'm working with some of the major players in the re-insurance market,' he says. 'If

Underhill: dared to dream of a career in re-insurance

you told me ten – even five – years ago that one day I would be working alongside the likes of Paul Elhorne, Michael Sorrenson and Selina Bourke, I wouldn't have believed you. Sometimes I have to pinch myself when I think about it!'

And his family is coming around to the idea. 'Sure, my wife and my parents were disappointed at first, but now they understand this is a passion for me and, just as an artist must paint, so must I build a broad client base of major reinsurance corporations.'

Matthew Taylor

YEAH ...
WHAT HE SAID !

The Chaser

Bush launches 'first strike' against terrorism sponsors: destroys CIA HQ

WASHINGTON, Monday: US President George W. Bush today ordered the first of many devastating pre-emptive attacks when he unleashed the full force of America's nuclear arsenal upon the CIA. The CIA's headquarters in Langley, Virginia were completely obliterated by the blitz, launched in response to evidence that the CIA has trained and funded terrorist groups for decades.

'From General Noriega and the Contra rebels to the elements which eventually became al-Qaeda, the CIA has consistently been closely affiliated with the world's most nefarious terrorist cells,' announced Bush. 'And in today's world, we simply can't afford to sit back and wait for them to attack us.'

Bush described the pre-emptive strike as particularly urgent given the CIA's access to weapons of mass destruction. While he regretted the massive

All that remains of the CIA's HQ in Langley, Virginia

lost of civilian life in the Virginia region as a result of the fallout from the attacks, Bush pointed out that such attacks would not have been necessary had the local population overthrown the CIA earlier.

The assault is only the first example of new US policy which dictates action be taken against the supporters of terrorism on a 'first strike' basis.

Secretary of Defence Donald Rumsfeld has already hinted at a forthcoming attack on the FBI, who he described as 'virtually helping out al-Qaeda, given the vast scale of their bumbling incompetence.'

'We also have reason to believe that my Israel policies may be actively encouraging the creation of Palestinian terrorist cells,' announced Rumsfeld, 'So I'll be taking immediate action against myself.'

While Rumsfeld flagged suspicions that several nations were possible terrorist safe havens, he admitted, 'Intelligence has been pretty hard to come by since the CIA exploded in a fireball.'

As an act of support for America's position, Australia last night destroyed ASIO's headquarters by crashing several Blackhawk helicopters into it.

Rumsfeld announces America's upcoming attack on the FBI

'Oliver!' cast concerned mufti Fridays will alter look of show

SYDNEY, Monday: A producer's plan for cast members of the hit musical *Oliver!* to perform every Friday in mufti has been criticised by theatre purists, who believe casual attire will detract from the show's period authenticity.

Under the proposal, principal singers and chorus members will be permitted to wear casual dress on Friday night performances throughout the production's run.

The architect of the plan said he believes mufti Fridays will lift the morale and productivity of his performance staff. 'Research shows that in industries across the board, employees relate much better to one another when they're loosened from the constraints of a uniform or specified dress code,' he said. 'Musical theatre's no different. Why should my staff be forced to wear the same costume every night? It's not good for

workplace dynamics.'

But opponents of the proposal are concerned the shift to casual wear on Fridays will alter the overall look and feel of the show. The production's costume designer is worried audiences won't be transported to Victorian London when the entire cast is in cargo pants.

'And what's more,' she asked, 'who's going to buy that Oliver's an orphan when he's getting about in a designer tank top and Reebok trainers? And Fagin's image as a panhandling ruffian will be shot to pieces if you ever see the poncy wardrobe of the actor playing him.'

An industry spokesman said a similar mufti plan at a leading amusement theme park was recently scuttled, after it became clear visitors took much less of a shine to the actors playing Mickey Mouse and Goofy when they weren't wearing the suit.

Mufti Oliver (right, with phat sunglasses), says he wants 'More', while his casually attired orphanage mates look on

Gustav Prinz: sick of people pointing to coincidental similarities between his autobiography and his own life

Writer denies drawing on own life for autobiography

SYDNEY, Thursday: An internationally acclaimed writer has dismissed reader speculation that his latest autobiography borrows heavily from his own life.

Longtime admirers of the writer Gustav Prinz said it was impossible to read his new memoir without concluding that it was deeply autobiographical.

Critics too have observed similarities between the autobiography's central figure and Prinz himself.

'For a start, both are called Prinz,' noted one reviewer. 'They were both born in the same German town, to the same mother. They both turn out to be writers. I mean, come on – the similarities are subtle, sure, but they're there.'

However the writer himself insists that the book, entitled *Gustav Prinz: My Life*, is in no way autobiographical. He described it as a work of the imagination, and said the events described in the book owed absolutely nothing to his own personal experience.

'If people want to read autobiographical parallels into this autobiography, well, fine. Good luck to them. But that wasn't my intention,' he said.

'I find the same thing happens every time I write something. People always say it must be about me. I remember ten years ago when I kept a diary, and everyone who read it was totally convinced it was all about my day-to-day life.'

SOCCER CONVERT TURNS DOWN INVITE TO WATCH LOCAL GAME

SYDNEY, Friday: A self-proclaimed soccer convert, who says the World Cup has made her fall in love with the sport, last night turned down a friend's invitation to watch a local club game.

The enthusiastic new fan has barely missed a game of the World Cup tournament, regularly packing into crowded pubs to soak up the atmosphere and watch all the action.

The young woman proclaimed that soccer was definitely her favourite football code, and that she deemed it to be a much more skilful and exciting game than either rugby or AFL.

But when a friend from work suggested that she come along with him to watch a local NSL game, she declined the invitation, nervously citing 'another engagement.'

The woman said her failure to attend the local match didn't mean that she wasn't still a hell-bent soccer

One of Australia's newest soccer converts

fanatic. She told her friend that she'd love to see a local game 'at some point down the track.'

By way of proving her passion for the sport, the woman even listed the names of all the players she's learnt during the World Cup. 'I can name Beckham, Ronaldo and, um...oh gee, who's that other one beginning with R?'

O.Watts

Subscribe to The Chaser

Get *The Chaser* newspaper home delivered. We guarantee that if it's not there in 30 minutes, we'll keep your money anyway.

The material in this book has been plagiarised from *The Chaser* newspaper, Australia's leading satirical journal. *The Chaser* is published every two weeks, or sometimes fortnightly, whichever comes first. Subscribers to *The Chaser* enjoy a large number of benefits:

* Get to read jokes while they're still topical, unlike in this book * Get something in their letterbox besides Thai takeaway menus * Get additional unsolicited post, after we've on-sold your address to a direct marketing mail list * FREE plastic covering with every *Chaser* posted to you * Huge discounts at cinemas and bookstores (offer ends Oct. 2002)

To subscribe to *The Chaser*, simply go to our website at www.chaser.com.au. Or fill out the form below (photocopies are acceptable, but please – no office Christmas party arses) and send to:

Chaser Subscriptions
Reply Paid 81515
PO Box 293
Darlinghurst, NSW, 1300

Have *The Chaser* delivered to your letterbox. By subscribing now, you save roughly $30,000 on the cost of setting up your own independent fortnightly newspaper. That's a saving of 150,000 %

SUBSCRIPTION FORM

SEND TO –

Chaser subscriptions
Reply paid 81515
PO Box 293
Darlinghurst NSW 1300
or Fax us on: 02-9356-8591

☐ **$25.00** (ten editions – six months)

☐ **$45.00** (twenty editions – one year)

☐ **$90.00** institutional (twenty editions – six months)

make cheques or money orders out to Chaser Publishing Pty Ltd

OR... Please debit my credit card

☐ Visa ☐ Mastercard ☐ Bankcard ☐ Amex: code _____

Name: _____

Address: _____

_____ Postcode: _____

Phone: _____ Email: _____

Expiry: ___ / ___

cardholder name: _____

cardholder signature: _____